Good Citizenship
and Educational Provision

This book is due for return on or before the last date shown below.

What ... of
influen... p
and wh... s
of teac...

Citi...
tempo...
meani...
our ri... s
book, ... e
what t... e
nature ... e
done t... s-
cussio... n
progra... p
educat... e
read b...

Ian D...
Unive... or
and u... e
admin...

Good Citizenship and Educational Provision

Ian Davies, Ian Gregory and Shirley C. Riley

London and New York

First published 1999
by Falmer Press
11 New Fetter Lane, London EC4P 4EE

Simultaneously published in the USA and Canada
by Garland Inc.
19 Union Square West, New York, NY 10003

Falmer Press is an imprint of the Taylor & Francis Group

© 1999 Ian Davies, Ian Gregory and Shirley C. Riley

Typeset in Times by
BC Typesetting, Bristol
Printed and bound in Great Britain by
Biddles Ltd, Guildford and King's Lynn

British Library Cataloguing in Publication Data
A catalogue record for this book is available from the British Library

Library of Congress Cataloguing in Publication Data
Davies, Ian, 1957–
    Good citizenship and educational provision/Ian Davies, Ian
Gregory, and Shirley C. Riley.
        p.   cm.
    Includes bibliographical references (p.) and index.
    1. Citizenship–Study and teaching–Great Britain.   2. Teachers–
Great Britain–Attitudes.   I. Gregory, Ian, 1939– .   II. Riley,
Shirley C., 1949– .   III. Title.
    LC1091.D28   1999
    372.83′2–dc21   99-28038

ISBN 0–7507–0960–X (hbk)
ISBN 0–7507–0959–6 (pbk)

Contents

Contents

Tables

Acknowledgements

The book could not have been written without the help of very many people. Principal among the people who should be thanked is Jeff Fouts of Seattle Pacific University, Washington, USA who co-ordinated the multi-nation research project of which the England study was just a part. Jeff Fouts also helped greatly with the analysis of data. Colleagues in the multi-national group have been extremely helpful in suggesting new approaches. Mention should be made in particular of Carol Stuen, who not only helped enormously with the production of statistical analysis of some of the research data but also suggested some valuable improvements during one of the early presentations of the findings at the British Educational Research Association (BERA) annual conference at the University of York (UK) in 1997. Warren Prior of Deakin University, Australia, offered valuable comments at various points, including at BERA 1997. Ken Fogelman of the University of Leicester, Colleen McLaughlin of Cambridge University and Don Rowe of the Citizenship Foundation, London, were extremely helpful in locating many of the schools that contributed data. The teachers who gave so freely of their time to supply us with data during a time of demanding widespread reform in England are thanked for their generosity and professionalism. Graham Vulliamy of the Department of Educational Studies at the University of York offered valuable advice on the research process at various points. Derek Heater gave very valuable feedback on an early version of Chapter 1. Liz Foster of Oxford University, in her role as editor of the Special Issue on political education of the *Oxford Review of Education* (1999), also offered very useful feedback on an earlier draft of Chapter 1. That journal is thanked for its permission to include material here in a slightly revised form from the original. Members of the Department of Educational Studies at the University of York offered useful feedback in a research seminar during a presentation made by Ian Gregory. We hope that the teachers and others will find the work reported here to be of use in their determination to provide citizenship education. Finally, the authors would like to make some personal acknowledgements for a great deal of support from Jim Riley and Lynn, Matthew, Hannah and Rachael Davies.

Introduction

This book seeks, in three main Parts, to:

- Characterize the main features of citizenship education in recent decades, a time during which it has been shifted through various forms and has attracted varying degrees of support.
- Discuss the main issues arising from a recently completed research project that involved the collection and analysis of data from over 700 teachers in England. This research focused on good citizenship. Principally, we wanted to know more about teachers' perceptions of good citizenship, their views about the key influences on and threats to the development of good citizenship, and their opinions of what can be done to help promote good citizenship.
- Make recommendations for practice in two broad areas: first, the development and implementation of curriculum initiatives in schools; and second, the specific actions which might be taken in programmes of initial and continuing teacher education.

An initial sketch of some key issues is necessary. Citizenship is undeniably important for reasons that are both intrinsic and to do with its current high-profile position on the political agenda. Dahrendorf has described the 1990s as 'the decade of the citizen' and there is no shortage of comment by prominent politicians and authors of international research and development projects which seek to understand and promote education for citizenship. These developments will be explored at various points in the book. The work reported here is timely as an increasing number of publications examine the meaning of citizenship education and how it has been and should be developed in the future (e.g. Cogan and Derricott 1998; Ichilov 1998). The fundamental, intrinsic importance of citizenship can be simply outlined. Crick's (QCA 1998) characterization of citizenship education, which has recently achieved support from the Secretary of State for Education and Employment, suggests that there are:

three things, related to each other, mutually dependent on each other, but each needing a somewhat different place and treatment in the curriculum . . . Firstly, children learning from the very beginning self confidence and socially and morally responsible behaviour both in and beyond the classroom, both towards those in authority and towards each other . . . Secondly, learning about and becoming helpfully involved in the life and concerns of their communities, including learning through community involvement and service to the community . . . Thirdly, pupils learning about and how to make themselves effective in public life through knowledge, skills and values what can be called 'political literacy', seeking for a term that is wider than political knowledge alone.

(QCA 1998, pp. 11–13)

Citizenship itself encompasses vitally important questions and issues. Heater (1990) has suggested that five key perspectives are significant in the debates that surround citizenship education: identity; civil citizenship; political citizenship; social citizenship; and civic virtue. Each of those perspectives is given some brief elaboration below.

Identity

The way in which people see themselves or are seen by others is important for citizenship. To be a citizen normally means that one belongs to a particular group. This may have legal connotations and there may be issues related to perceptions of nationhood. This may mean that citizenship can be expressed in very specific and concrete terms, with the possibility that we can clearly distinguish between those who are or who are not citizens in certain circumstances. It can lead to recourse to law to attempt to ensure that rights and responsibilities are enforced. Even within this characterization there are disagreements about who is a citizen. Of course, it may also lead to profound disagreements if the nature of identity is perceived to relate more to a sense of individual or group belonging, which in some way goes beyond more narrow legalistic interpretations. The call for us to be citizens of the world has been heard. There is clear evidence of people identifying more strongly, for example, with local or gender groups than with national states; and at times it becomes hard to see clear differences between the terms 'citizen' and 'person'.

Civil Citizenship

Although the comments made above referred to potential legal implications of identity, the area of civil citizenship is less problematically bound up with the nature of the law. There are rights for certain people in certain countries to property, trial by jury, recourse to appeal and so on. There will always be debates surrounding the interplay between law and justice, and the ever-burgeoning case law means that this area will always be fluid. There may, however, be in practice, even if not explicitly stated, a bedrock of agreed understanding within which the legal rights of citizens are considered.

Political Citizenship

Most British citizens over the age of 18 have the right to vote. There are a number of formally excluded groups such as prisoners, the Royal Family and those suffering from certain sorts of illness; but some would argue that there are also groups which, while not being formally excluded, are effectively excluded. This exclusion could relate both to issues of voting (some individuals and groups are less likely to vote than others) and to issues of representation (in Britain today there are proportionally very few women and black MPs and very few MPs with disabilities). Discussions over the question of whether voting is a right or a duty, whether the system of voting is fair, whether local or national or other structures are most effective for the exercise of citizenship and the relative merits of the, broadly stated, 'system' of democracy (for example, representative or participatory) which should be preferred are some of the issues which are significant in the field of political citizenship.

Social Citizenship

In the Cold War era there seemed to be, if we were to argue simplistically, some sort of distinction between political citizenship in the West and social citizenship in the East. Social citizenship, of course, does find some expression in many countries and is to do with, generally, the fight to ensure that all citizens have access to acceptable levels of health, education and living standards. Thus economic factors (and, perhaps, some would make a case for a somewhat distinct economic citizenship) are significant. Discussion about issues in this area is of relatively recent origin. The main debates concern the level of provision that should be made available and the ways in which those services should be offered. This usually includes debates over the arrangements for paying for the services, deciding upon the eligibility of those who will benefit from the provision, and what generally this means in terms of societies being more or less paternalist or egalitarian.

Civic Virtue

Some, and perhaps all, of the above characterizations of citizenship involve action taken by individuals and groups but it is in the area of civic virtue that debates raise most explicitly issues about community service and other forms of contributing actively to an immediate improvement of social conditions. These debates have been particularly prominent in Britain since at least the 1980s, although there is a long tradition of searching for the most effective ways to make progress. That, however, does not mean that the area is without controversy. The very term 'community service' used above is felt by some to be inappropriate. For young people's work to begin to take the place of state action is potentially problematic if the motives are even unintentionally associated with saving money by exploiting idealism in the establishment of programmes which are only superficially educational and inherently conservative.

The above characterizations of citizenship are not exhaustive. There are other notions or, at least, other perspectives on citizenship which have not been mentioned. No reference has been made to, for example, feminist citizenship, postmodern citizenship or religious citizenship. But what the above characterizations do indicate is that citizenship is a complex and shifting field. Fouts (1997) has suggested that citizenship is dependent upon contemporary individual and societal considerations relating to geography and culture, is an essentially contested concept (to use W. B. Gallie's (1964) phrase) rooted in fundamental philosophical differences, and is determined at least in part by historical circumstances. This does not mean, however, that we must forever be lost in a postmodernist maze. Rather, it suggests that there is a need to explore the issues in a way which will lead to conceptual clarification, to a greater understanding of what sorts of teacher education are needed, and what teachers and others can do when working with young people.

The debates relating to citizenship in this book which have been briefly mentioned above, have been considered and given a particular focus through the work of Gross and Dynneson (e.g. Gross and Dynneson 1991; Dynneson 1992). These authors have referred to the complexities of citizenship, focused on the 'good citizen' and explained that that is 'a label commonly used to describe people who consistently do the right thing according to a formal or informal list of values and behaviors' (Dynneson 1992, p. 55). The use of the term 'good citizenship' used in this book reflects the influence of those authors and we believe that by identifying these behaviours a clearer understanding and operationalization of the concept of good citizenship will be possible. Gross and Dynneson have undertaken some valuable research work on this theme with secondary students in the United States. The present authors wanted to see how far it would be possible to understand more about teachers' understandings of citizenship. It was hoped that this would make it possible to aid curriculum reform. If there were gaps between the theorists in the area of citizenship education and the conceptions of teachers this had to be known to make curriculum development and reform implementation more possible.

The inspiration and practical means which drove this work was a multi-nation research project co-ordinated by Professor Jeff Fouts of Seattle Pacific University. This project explored the varying understandings of citizenship in a number of countries. The results of the research from all participating countries will be reported elsewhere (Fouts forthcoming); the results of the work arising from data collection and analysis in England and the consequent recommendations are presented in this book.

It needs to be stated clearly that the authors have a very positive and constructive view of the possible relationships between the concerns of citizenship and education. In so many areas of citizenship we find deep parallels. Principal figures in politics (such as Plato, Locke and Rousseau) are not by accident also writers on education. Further:

> There is evidence that aspects of formal education are certainly relevant to political identity, expertise and participation. Formal politics or civic education does make some difference; relevant propositional knowledge and skill are also gained (or not) elsewhere in the curriculum; classroom practice impacts on values and on levels of political participation; the organization of school governance also seems relevant. The widespread judgements that levels of voter turnout, other political and civic participation and commitment to democratic values is too low or too fragile either in populations in general or in younger birth cohorts in particular has turned the attention of governments, educators, philosophers and others to the project of improving political education in schools and in other institutions.
>
> (Foster 1999, p. 12)

A SUMMARY OF THE BOOK

The book, as explained above, is divided into three main Parts. These are interrelated but the chapters have been written to allow the reader to select areas of particular interest. Indeed, although the recommendations which are made in the later chapters refer to the research project around which this book is focused, we do not pretend that we have somehow emerged with a set of objectively correct answers to the complex issues and questions which surround citizenship education.

Part I consists of one chapter on the recent history of education for citizenship. It aims to place the research project and issues arising from it in a proper context. There is discussion of four models of political learning:

- The British Constitution approach, used in academic courses with students who were perceived as being of high ability. These courses were often the only form of political learning available prior to the 1960s. The focus was usually on 'Whitehall and town hall'.

- Political literacy approaches perhaps were more a characteristic of the late 1960s and 1970s. They included a greater interest in skills, issues and developing students' potential for action. The framework encompassed a view of politics as being that which extended far beyond constitutions. This view acknowledged the immediate politics that operate in such contexts as the youth club and trade union as being of great significance.

- During the 1980s a group of 'new' or 'adjectival' educations came to prominence. An umbrella term for these many new approaches could be 'global education'. Global education was characterized by affective learning and holistic approaches to world issues. The many 'educations' which were related to this approach included anti-racist education, peace education, anti-sexist education.

- Citizenship education has been a significant feature of attempts to provide political learning during the 1990s. It is currently the subject of controversy. Citizenship itself is a contested concept and the aims and methods which are associated with education for citizenship are still under review.

Within the above models there are three important strands. First, illustration of the models, wherever possible, will be made by reference to particular initiatives. Examples are given for some of the models, but it is also important to note that there is relative lack of practical examples and projects which can be discussed in this chapter. The reasons for the very significant failure to implement coherent or widespread programmes of political learning are raised. Second, there is the (loosely phrased) 'geopolitical' orientation of the models: in other words, the point on the personal–local–regional–national–international spectrum on which the models can be located. There is some discussion of the way in which the models juxtapose areas that are potentially dichotomous: for example, the personal with the public, the national with the European, the local with the global. The third strand explores the educational orientation of the models. In this strand the relative importance of knowledge, skills and dispositions are probed. The perceived preferred level of critical engagement by students is considered in an attempt to evaluate the underlying intended purpose and likely outcome of initiatives associated with each model.

Part II contains four chapters and explores the methods and findings of the research project. In Chapter 2, 'Researching Teachers' Perceptions of Good Citizenship and Educational Provision', the methods used in the research project are discussed. We do not give an unnecessarily detailed account which would involve long discussion of, for example, the methods used to undertake valid statistical analysis. However, if the reader is to have a reasonable opportunity to evaluate the claims being made in this book, some account must be given of our research methods. The methods are described and explained in terms which are deliberately written in a style intended to reach the interested general reader as well as the professional (itself a relevant commitment in a book aiming to promote support for citizenship education). The following are given explicit attention:

- the context in which the research took place
- the key research questions and the way in which they were generated
- the construction of the sample of teachers, the development of question-naire and interview schedules
- the way in which analysis of data led to conclusions.

This methodological outline has the additional intended benefit of encouraging and guiding others, in the spirit of constructive partnership, who wish to undertake their own investigations into the nature of education for citizenship, without the authors wishing to suggest that there cannot be useful alternative strategies to those they discuss.

In Chapter 3, 'What Do Teachers Mean by Good Citizenship?', there is the first presentation of findings from the research project. Teachers' views about good citizenship are explored and three key areas are discussed:

1   Social concern: i.e. concern for the welfare of others; moral and ethical behaviour; tolerance of diversity within society.
2   Knowledge: i.e. knowledge of government; knowledge of current events; knowledge of the world community; ability to question ideas.
3   Conservatism: i.e. acceptance of those in a supervisory role; patriotism; acceptance of assigned responsibilities.

A number of important points emerge from the discussion. There is a huge gap between the views of those academics who have produced models of citizenship and the views of teachers on the nature of citizenship. While this difference is not necessarily or entirely negative, it does suggest that both 'sides' should be helped to become more aware of the other's position. If this exchange of knowledge were achieved, teachers might come to have a more informed understanding of key issues. There will also be the potential for replacing certain models of curriculum change based on the ideas emerging from expert but rather closed working parties, by the development of a more realistic and targeted strategy which derives from an understanding of teachers' thinking.

The use of categories such as 'conservativism' should not be taken to imply that the teachers are in fact conservative. Rather, these categories allow for a discussion of the way in which teachers explain their thinking. Very generally, teachers rate social concern characteristics positively, and see in particular the importance of local community-based action to help others; they give some rather limited support to the notion of knowledge being important for citizenship; they react negatively to certain ideas and practices associated with the very broad concept of patriotism and, in their wish to adhere to rules, stress the significance of justice over law.

In Chapter 4, 'Teacher Perceptions of the Key Influences upon the Development of Good Citizenship', we explore the ways in which teachers perceive the development of citizenship. At times, teachers talked about the influences which were most personally significant. Given the broad characterization of citizenship that teachers work with, it is important to probe their perceptions of the ways in which citizenship can be gained, enhanced and how it may be threatened. The aim of this work is to make more possible the development of curriculum implementation strategies and frameworks. If, for example, certain elements were considered by teachers to be highly influential in developing good citizenship, then it would seem important for curriculum developers to give those features proper consideration. This discussion would make it possible to move beyond a situation in which society simplistically expects teachers to produce good citizens. The most influential group by far is deemed to be parents, with other important influences said to be friends, teachers, extracurricular activities and siblings. The most significant factor or issue perceived as being most threatening to good citizenship is by far drugs, closely followed by negative role models, family conflicts and peer pressure. Of course, it seems curious that little has been raised about the contribution to be made by the subject matter of lessons on citizenship. These points may lead both to a refocusing of energy by curriculum reformers on, for example, the relationship between schools and families and, generally, a new way of introducing citizenship education and evaluating its impact. Some greater attention to citizenship education may also be required in the continuing professional development of teachers, so that they are more ready to assert, plan for and teach effective citizenship education through explicitly targeted lessons.

These sorts of issues are explored further in Chapter 5, 'What Sort of Work Do Teachers Believe Should Take Place in Schools to Promote Good Citizenship?'. Teachers have been asked to give their views on the nature of programmes for good citizenship. This leads to a consideration of whether there are in fact a number of citizenships: those for children (or perhaps certain kinds of school pupil) and those for the adult in the local community. During the last few decades it has been proposed that relevant learning can take place through academic subjects, cross-curricular lessons, such as Personal and Social Education (PSE), and the ethos of the school or hidden curriculum, and by means of involving pupils in local community projects. An evaluation of the approaches mentioned above used in schools helps to assess the likelihood of achieving real and effective as opposed to phantom programmes. The latter are those which head teachers refer to when faced with a government official wanting to know what is being done in the name of education for citizenship. It seems entirely consistent with the teachers' views on the meaning of the good citizen that community projects are emphasized as being a valuable way forward. It is slightly confusing, given teachers' views about the meaning of the good citizen as a person who takes action to support individuals in the local community (but not necessarily a contradiction), that they also recommend international projects. Again, there is the possibility that a number of different characterizations of citizenship are operating at the same time, with a need for teachers perhaps to be more aware of those potential inconsistencies seems necessary.

Part III, 'What Is To Be Done? Ways Forward in the Development of Good Citizenship through Education', has two chapters. The purpose of Part III is to develop some recommendations that can carry citizenship education forward. That said, it is, of course, necessary to ensure that a clear distinction is to be made between research findings and recommendations. The authors of this book are clearly not in a position to be able to know what will work in any particular school or setting. Chapter 6, 'Action in Schools', gives a range of recommendations relating to the action that might be taken by curriculum planners and also by a variety of teachers within schools. The reader is asked to consider specific plans for action in three main ways:

- the means by which working parties on the curriculum can operate to ensure that the development of frameworks given to teachers are those which they (i.e. teachers) can work with positively
- the structures that can be used within schools by heads and senior teachers which may enable positive action to take place
- the work to be undertaken by individual teachers.

Chapter 7, 'Action in Programmes of Initial Teacher Education and Continuing Professional Development', explores vitally important areas that have been transformed by central government in England and elsewhere in recent years. The government sees teacher education as one of the principal means by which standards can be raised. This chapter reviews the recent and likely future changes in this field and makes recommendations for policy makers, serving teachers and those hoping to enter the profession to ensure that there will be a workforce which has been empowered to undertake necessary initiatives in citizenship education. Three overarching areas of contacts and resources, access to teacher education, and a process of teacher education which is appropriate to citizenship education are discussed. Also, three more specific issues are explored, with some discussion of the approach which could be adopted towards the development of teachers' knowledge, teaching and assessing.

Chapter 8, 'Conclusions', gives a summary of what the book has argued and what needs to be done. Arguments are made for giving citizenship education a guaranteed place in any statutory curriculum and for the programme to be detailed and realistic. Although we remain rather sceptical as to the prospects for citizenship education, it is recognized that there are more grounds for optimism now than at almost any other time. The dispositions of teachers, the strong interest in citizenship as an area of academic debate and the recent high profile it has enjoyed among politicians in England and elsewhere mean that something can be done.

Part I

Good Citizenship and Educational Provision in Context

1 The Recent History of Citizenship Education

INTRODUCTION

This chapter begins with a brief historical sketch of some relevant events and trends. We then argue that there have been three main periods of citizenship education in schools during the last three decades. Political literacy, which was in a dominant position in the 1970s, was succeeded in the 1980s by a wide array of 'new' or 'adjectival' educations which ranged from peace to global and from anti-sexist to anti-racist education. These were in turn supplanted more recently by a direct focus on citizenship education. A description of each of these main phases is given. Prior to a brief conclusion, we discuss four key trends with some comments about future prospects.

Before the above can be tackled, however, it is necessary to make clear the parameters of the chapter. The time period under review is almost entirely restricted to 1969 (the year when the Politics Association was established) to the present; the geographical focus is England; and, generally, only issues relating to schools are discussed (and largely those for pupils in the compulsory years of secondary education in the state sector). The nature of citizenship explored here is restricted. Although some mention is made of other factors, the focus of the work relates to those deliberate efforts to promote knowledge, understanding, skills and the potential for action, and to support pupils' dispositions which are congruent with living within (rather than merely studying) a democratic society. There is a stronger emphasis on political aspects of citizenship education than on other related but potentially distinct fields, such as moral education. Although some mention is made of a number of centrally important related fields, citizenship education is not seen as covering everything that might aim at a better society and, indeed, the terms 'political education' and 'citizenship education' are often used in the chapter interchangeably. Examples from specific and potentially relevant areas such as history education are not given detailed attention. While this omission is partly due to limitations of space, it also reflects two other important points: that there are remarkably few concrete and explicit examples of citizenship education programmes in mainstream schools and colleges which could be referred to; and, while we strongly hope that a better world can be made at least in part through education, any programme must be realistic and limited. This latter important point is developed more fully in the conclusion to the book.

BRIEF HISTORICAL BACKGROUND

If the discussion within the last three decades is to mean anything, it must be placed within some sort of context. Heater (1977a), Brennan (1981) and Batho (1990) have charted the historical developments in some detail. This historical material makes for rather depressing reading. The Spens (Board of Education 1928) and Norwood (Board of Education 1943) Reports largely neglect the area, reflecting the failure of the Association for Education in Citizenship (Whitmarsh 1974), and although the 1944 Education Act included a clause favourable to political education (Brennan 1981, p. 40), this was never implemented. Although some support was given from time to time to Commonwealth Studies, pamphlets issued in 1947 (Ministry of Education 1947) and 1949 (Ministry of Education 1949) concentrate on the British Constitution for any reference to political education, and the latter illogically suggests that a 'healthy democratic society' could be encouraged if schools would only develop 'the old and simple virtues of humility, service, restraint and respect for personality' (p. 41). The Crowther Report (Ministry of Education 1959) is largely silent on the matter of political learning, the Newsom Report (Ministry of Education 1963) does make a claim about the importance of educating children so that they are not the victims of the 'hidden persuaders' (p. 163) but there is no thorough consideration of the topic. Traditional school subjects such as history (DES 1967) were felt to be the area in which political education would find expression rather than through the development of any explicit and systematic approach. Some Schools Council papers (e.g. 1967) make passing references to political education but fail to give any in-depth treatment and are themselves part of the expression of neglect which led to most pupils having: 'little good to say for what they have learnt in those subjects which are concerned with the understanding of human nature and institutions' (Schools Council 1967, para. 62).

Of course, there are exceptions that could be made to this general picture. Those interested in citizenship education before 1969 were able to draw (positively or negatively) from the work of Dewey (1916/1966), Laski (1934) and Oakshott (1956). Some relevant research and development work had taken place (e.g. Oliver and Shaver 1966) and the Association for the Teaching of Social Sciences had been set up in 1963. Very important has been the long-term existence of the Council for Education in World Citizenship (Heater 1983).

However, in general, before 1969, if any citizenship education was being promoted it was largely almost exclusively for elite students (e.g. those studying at HSC or 'A' level), and was based around acquiring information for the purposes of doing well academically and preparing for high-status professions. If it was ever practised in any explicit sense for majorities, it was as civics which 'may have been utopian, quietist, simplistic, indoctrinating as well as class biased, hardly meriting the description of "education"' (Entwistle 1973, p. 7).

This low level of implementation seems to have continued. There has in fact been very little explicit work undertaken in schools. Even high-status policy initiatives do not translate easily into classroom practice. This has been a consistent finding of those who searched for evidence of political education in recent decades. Stradling and Noctor (1981) and Fogelman (1991) both report positively on what head teachers say when faced with an official-looking questionnaire, but the reality is, they argue, rather more prosaic. Even Stradling and Noctor's estimate that the average pupil will receive no more than two 35-minute periods per week of political education for no more than 10 weeks of the year seems optimistic (Davies 1993a). Lister's use of the term 'phantom curriculum' to describe what is happening seems entirely appropriate. The half-formed expectation was that citizenship education would be somehow the job of the history teacher, the subject of a few assemblies, a module in a PSE programme taught by someone drafted to fill in spaces on a 'proper' subject's timetable, which would not be assessed and would not be seriously evaluated through inspection (whatever the current rhetoric from Ofsted). There are, of course, exceptions, and teachers struggling with excessive administrative burdens often contrive small-scale wonders (e.g. Davies et al. 1998), but the general picture is unimpressive.

Heater (1977b) has explained the reasons for the neglect: a lack of tradition; few teachers who were professionally committed to the field; a belief that politics was solely an adult domain; and a fear of indoctrination. It is true that from the 1960s the situation began to change in relation to the attention given to political education by policy makers, and four factors are described in the next section to explain the transformation.

THE REASONS FOR THE EMERGENCE OF POLITICAL EDUCATION DURING THE 1970s

First, the lowering of the age of majority to 18 in 1970 had a significant impact. For the first time, sixth formers and others in full-time education would be allowed to vote. For them to have had no formal experience of political education seemed an anomaly. Second, work relating to political socialisation, either generally (e.g. Dawson et al. 1977), or that which focused specifically on children and what particular ideas they could cope with (Jahoda 1963; Greenstein 1965; Connell 1971), or through an examination of the nature of school textbooks and their potential impact (Gilbert 1984) was important. The notion that politics was something that children knew nothing about, and should at best be left to be discussed within the private world of families, could now be dispelled. Political messages were contained in school texts, and children could understand political concepts. As such, there was some acceptance of the need for political education to be undertaken more explicitly.

Third, although it is always hard to judge the extent of political ignorance among young people, key politicians took note of research which carried alarming messages (Stradling 1977) and were keen to 'edge young people away from the margins of politics into the mainstream' (Stradling 1987, p. 3). Finally, the late 1960s and early 1970s saw a number of studies and reforms all associated with the democratization of educational structures. Kerckhoff et al. (1996) and Chitty and Benn (1996) have recently discussed the growing school population, the interest in equality, dissatisfaction with intelligence tests, the presence of an expanding number of young teachers and a greater concern with reforms of process as well as content, which would mean that the political nature of education would be stressed. Research studies which stressed the importance of structural and personal relationships were prominent during this period and were clearly seen to be relevant to the need to develop political understanding (e.g. Hargreaves 1972). With the climate of public – or, at least, professional – opinion influenced by radical thinking (e.g. Reimer 1975), it became increasingly difficult not to accept that politics had to be included in the curriculum. The nature of what, precisely, was meant by 'politics' was not clarified at that point but, as shown below, various concepts became relatively clear during the development of different notions during the following decades.

TYPES OF CITIZENSHIP EDUCATION PROMOTED DURING THE PERIOD 1969–1999

Although it is not possible neatly to encapsulate all the many initiatives taken during the last few decades into coherent groupings, we argue that there are essentially three main (overlapping) frameworks which can be discussed: political literacy; 'new' or 'adjectival' educations and education for citizenship. For each of these frameworks we attempt to describe the key features, explain why they came about and why (at least for the first two) they faded.

Political Literacy – from Thinking about Politics to Political Issues

The Programme for Political Education (PPE) had as its key aim political literacy. PPE was supported by the Hansard Society. Many of its leading advocates had a strong and positive relationship with the Politics Association, which had been established in 1969. The principal figure was Bernard Crick. There was a critical approach to knowledge and efforts were made to ensure that pupils could learn about politics (in various contexts). The goal was to make people critically aware and potentially more active for life in a society that could be more than nominally democratic.

Political literacy made four main shifts away from earlier work. It was issue-focused; it used a broader concept of politics than had been used in British Constitution courses; it valued procedural concepts; and it was concerned with skills as well as knowledge and attitudes, so as to develop pupils' potential for action. The key publication was edited by Crick and Porter (1978). That book emerged from a series of conceptual working papers and research reports arising from six case studies of educational institutions which were developing new approaches to political education.

The central phase of the PPE was between 1974 and 1977, although work continued long after that point. It achieved high-status recognition with the explicit support of HMIs (who made statements in 1977 and 1979), and of the Secretary of State for Education (Humberside undated). In 1980 the DES produced *A Framework for the School Curriculum* and as a result the Politics Association commented that it welcomed: 'the specific inclusion of the "social and political" area of experience and the principle that all [areas of the curriculum] are of equal importance' (Brennan 1981, p. 142).

By the end of the 1970s, political literacy did seem to have gained a strong position with key policy makers. Legitimation had been achieved, however, without implementation and during the 1980s it was replaced by a raft of 'new' educations.

'New' or 'Adjectival' Educations – the Radical Agenda

The 'new' educations are perhaps not a coherent school of thought or action other than in the commitment they have to social justice. The relationship with citizenship education (as suggested in the conclusion to this book), is not necessarily always helpful or straightforward. Some, such as Peace Education and World Studies, had existed from the post-First World War era (Heater 1984); others, such as anti-sexist and anti-racist education, were more recent. Academics in 'new' areas such as women's studies, as well as trade unionists, workers for aid organizations and teachers, were regarded as being the ones involved in the promotion of projects as well as, at times, setting up departments in schools. These various camps often competed between themselves for resources and curriculum space.

There were a number of key shifts made after the work of the 1970s. First, whereas political literacy saw those from traditional academic subjects attempting to expand the nature of work on politics so that it had the potential for democratic understanding and action, the initiatives of the 1980s which, while for the most part had similarly democratic credentials, also had a harder edge and would not achieve the same level of support from key decision makers. Instead of having a broad framework of politics which was applied to issues that affected everyday lives, the new educations seemed to give more attention to specific issues. Supporters argued that those issues were both vitally important in themselves and that also there could be some way in which the specifics could be made to generate a more decent society.

There were a number of key issues but four were always more important than others: the bomb; gender; development; and 'race' (the latter in inverted commas as the very existence of 'race' is, in our view, to be challenged). All four areas were concerned with social justice and had a number of strengths. The issues were undeniably important. A number of local education authorities (e.g. Newcastle undated) gave a lead at a time when many perceived there to be grave dangers for world safety. Those active in these movements were reflecting wider debates and actions and were very much a part of the climate of the early 1980s which encompassed the 1978–9 'winter of discontent'; the 1981 riots in Liverpool, Bristol and London; reactions against the excesses of monetarist government policy and the controversies of Howe's 1981 budget; the teachers' strikes of the mid-1980s; and actions by women who were cultivating far more developed versions of what was needed for a just society than had been allowed for by the 1975 Sex Discrimination Act.

The teachers who became involved with such work were not (or at least not as obviously as those associated with previous initiatives) academics moving from high-status disciplines, making comments about teachers and schools. The new groups included many intelligent and creative teachers and the relative lack of emphasis (with some exceptions, e.g. see Crick and Porter 1978) by the advocates of political literacy on producing a teaching and learning programme (Stradling 1987) was now seen even more starkly as packs, books, guides and schemes of work were developed. Hicks' 1988 book, *Education for Peace*, has a subtitle which stresses action in the classroom; the work on world studies and later on global education by Pike and Selby (e.g. 1988), while always being academically respectable, is largely concerned with what teachers can actually do with children.

However, some of these strengths could also be seen as weaknesses and would mean that although much of this work continues in the 1990s in the form of, for example, education for the future (e.g. Hicks and Holden 1995;

Hicks 1994), there were serious problems about the overarching coherence of the ideas and the likelihood of these movements being accepted. Intellectually, the new educations were fragmented. This was not simply a matter of divisions between those favouring, for example, peace as opposed to another focal point. Rather, within each of the different camps there were very different conceptions. Conflict resolution, for example, can be seen as needing investigations into international crises and/or an exploration of the inner self (e.g. Kragh 1995). Feminism is a very broad church and the possibility for a united front between the different elements seems impossible (Bryson 1993). The shifts in other areas can be seen easily, with the multiculturalism of the 1970s being replaced by the anti-racist education of the 1980s, which in turn now seems to be replaced by intercultural education. Intellectual fragmentation and commitment to particular objectives which are perceived as being radical docs not lead to widespread acceptance. Rather, certain local education authorities became associated with what seemed to be party political aims. Peace education guidelines produced separately by Avon and Manchester were in some ways open to easy attack (Lister 1984). As Scruton (1985) attacked Pike and Selby, and Mary Warnock in her Dimbleby Lecture talked of the 'educational horror stories' that all parents tell, sections 44 and 45 of the 1986 Education Act (Number 2) were forbidding political activity in schools and requiring teachers in secondary schools to ensure that there was always a balanced presentation of opposing views. The new educations, however unfairly, were perceived now as edging young people towards the margins of politics rather than being the means of saving them from that fate. As such, despite all their strengths (particularly their acceptance by teachers and the continued use of the teaching materials in many schools and the ongoing development of theoretical and practical approaches, e.g. Steiner 1996) the radical agenda has simply faded from view. In the face of intellectual incoherence and an inability to withstand attack from well-placed political opponents, the debate has moved on to a consideration of the parameters of the National Curriculum and the primacy of literacy and numeracy.

Education for Citizenship – the Unresolved Agenda

The 1990s were seen at an early point, according to Dahrendorf, as being the 'decade of the citizen' (Keane 1990). Education for citizenship having been declared as one of the five cross-curricular themes of the National Curriculum (NCC 1990) and the subject of a report by the Commission on Citizenship (1990), it seemed that perhaps something would be done. For the period of the first half of the decade this expectation was soon shown to be unfilled. The cross-curricular themes have for various reasons (but mostly due to the pressure of other priorities introduced by demands of teaching and assessing the National Curriculum) been generally ignored

(Whitty et al. 1994). Indeed, of the five themes, education for citizenship seems to have been the one which is ignored most often. Although it is possible that new working groups (on values and on citizenship – the latter chaired by Crick – and with much valuable work done by the Citizenship Foundation) may develop a new impetus, this seems unlikely. The shift from use of the title 'education for citizenship' to 'citizenship education' seems to be an attempt to look for something more tightly targeted rather than merely assuming that positive results will emerge from a general input. But the government's current drive to raise standards in literacy and numeracy is unlikely to lead to a radical refocusing of energy onto this area. Although the chief executive of the Qualifications and Curriculum Authority (QCA) has recently explained that one of the purposes of a review of the National Curriculum will be to address citizenship education more adequately (Tate 1998), one of his own recent statements seems to give a realistic assessment of the difficulties of making radical shifts (Tate 1997).

Throughout this book, and in later chapters in particular, there is a determined effort to be constructive and positive and this includes raising possible new ways to conceptualize and activate citizenship education. However, the difficulties and obstacles need to be clearly understood if action is even to be seen as possible.

The National Curriculum Council (NCC) suggested eight essential components, comprising: community; pluralism; rights and responsibilities of citizens; specific explorations of the family; democracy in action; the citizen and the law; work and employment; and leisure and public services. The Commission on Citizenship (1990) report, although it included many valuable suggestions, became associated narrowly and negatively with the recommendation for more voluntary action by young people. The reasons for this particular form of citizenship education being promoted are not encouraging. It seems that demographic changes which mean that there is a greater proportion of older people not in paid work need desperate measures. The authors of this new form of education may be aware that, as Mulgan (1990, p. 9) suggests: 'welfarism is dying and the best way to prevent its resurrection is to replace it'. Other factors perceived as explaining the rise of citizenship education are similarly discouraging, and include such elements as the rising crime rate, the decline of local government and the consequent disappearance of safety nets for the less well off, the growth of consumerism and consumer education which shifted the agenda towards economics and away from politics, the influence of the new Europe with its emphasis on citizenship rights and obligations, and the desire to marry liberal and communitarian thought more closely (Davies 1994a).

The nature of citizenship education is similarly not encouraging. It is largely built upon an analysis developed by Marshall (1963), who argued that the development of legal, political and social rights in the last three centuries has led to our contemporary understandings and actions. Marshall's liberal approach which, by placing a strong emphasis on welfare rights, was (for its time) a relatively radical and positive view and would satisfy those who see politics as the process of conciliation of different groups and individuals. Marshall, however, does not suit all participants in the contemporary debates about citizenship. He can be criticized as being conservative in his arguments against 'any hasty attempt to reverse present and recent trends' (Marshall 1963, p. 127); in his suggestion of rights being granted rather than seized; in his acceptance of 'legitimate' inequalities; in his now out of date restriction of the debates surrounding citizenship which, at least by implication, excludes key groups such as women and black people and key issues such as identity; and, in his failure to provide any practical political agenda or pedagogical programme.

Carr (1991), in a potentially more politicized approach, has argued that the contemporary battle, at least in the first half of the 1990s, has been between different sections of the Right who wish either to promote the moral aspects (duty, responsibility, and often national identity) of citizenship or those who wish to emphasize the market model which stresses the needs of entrepreneurs and the benefits of enterprise.

It is important to take note of such issues and thus avoid an indifference towards very different conceptions of citizenship which could, on the one hand, be a kind of civic individualism in which, for example, a person secures a pension for him/herself; and, on the other, the politics of the common good in which citizenship is collective political effort in the context of social justice.

However, the recent QCA committee on education for citizenship, chaired by Bernard Crick (QCA 1998) has drawn in a limited way positively, and usefully, from the thinking of Marshall (although certain phrases in its initial report will need to be rewritten if there is to be a modern and more acceptable reflection of the multicultural society which could be targeted). Politics is seen as a process of conciliation and the three areas of 'social and moral responsibility, community involvement and political literacy' (p. 13) have been highlighted. Whether or not the committee's sensible recognition that 'a working definition [of citizenship education] must be wide' (p. 12) can still be meaningful as it tries to incorporate recent discussions about civic disengagement, morality and volunteering is not clear. If integration between these various elements is being sought it is possible that certain features favourable to the societal *status quo* may be supported. Volunteering, for example, despite the committee's best intentions may come to appear as being more significant than political literacy. This seems particularly likely if more practical pedagogical recommendations will exist only in terms of 'an output model alone' (p. 7). That is, although the learning outcomes are promised to be 'tightly defined' (p. 7) by the end of the committee's work, there will be no programmes of study or compulsory experiences. A necessary broad definition, coupled with a very sensible unwillingness to provide the perceived potential for political indoctrination, and a very welcome reluctance not to demand that teachers' actions are too tightly restrained or that they have too great a bureaucratic burden, may actually lead to little being done.

TRENDS AND PROSPECTS

Some attempt has been made above to explain not only what was happening in each of the three decades but also to say something about why those forms of education emerged. It is now necessary to develop a broader approach which can identify some of the trends apparent across the different projects.

It must be stressed that an objective account cannot be written. Interpretation based on comparative data will always lead to uncertainty. Two main reasons can be advanced to support this hesitation. First, we find it hard to distinguish between those statements which are merely ploys aimed at achieving a particular goal and, alternatively, those which are honestly intended to be a simple reflection of reality. Citizenship education does not differ from other educational initiatives which are themselves political projects. Those members of organizations who promote specific forms of teaching and learning do so for a variety of motives. The evidence that they use needs to be questioned. Second, the nature of what is being advocated or rejected will, of course, mean different things at different times to a variety of people. The consensus of the 1960s may be what we today would regard as authoritarian. Simple comparative history is unlikely ever to lead to more than superficial insights.

Nevertheless, the following account draws attention to a number of overarching and overlapping factors which demonstrate what has happened to citizenship education in schools over the last three decades.

Curriculum Reform Driven by a Sense of Crisis

There has always been greater interest in political learning at times of crisis (Stradling 1987; Marshall 1988). Gollancz and Somervell (1914), Stewart (1938) and Cole (1942) all attracted some attention at moments of crisis, and were perceived as voices in the wilderness at other points. Some of the crises since the 1970s have been referred to above. In many ways, they were real crises and political education benefited from them and perhaps even helped in minor ways to alleviate them. During the 1970s there was a fear of the growth of extremist organizations; in the 1980s the bomb and the unjust social exclusion of many, including women and black people, became particularly important; and, in the 1990s there has been a perceived need to reduce the crime rate and shore up the welfare state by increasing the voluntary activity of young people. The cry for urgent action can still be seen.

Marquand (1997) talks of the choice we must make sooner or later 'between the free market and the free society' (p. 33), and Fukuyama (1997) claims that we are living through the 'great disruption'. However, although there are some calls today for educational reform (and some of those calls are very relevant to the development of world citizenship, e.g. Nussbaum 1997), the climate in England is now more one of consensus in which the key targets are basic skills and increased examination success which may help develop economic performance. There may be evidence for continued low levels of civic engagement (Crewe et al. 1996), and there will always be those who refer to, and/or attempt to develop, moral panics but, as there is perceived not to be strong evidence for a generational decline of political interest and activity (Jowell and Park 1997), there are no very strong crisis cards to play. Indeed, even those who do believe that generational shifts have occurred do so only by arguing that: 'Rising levels of education and economic security seem to be producing a gradual intergenerational shift toward placing less emphasis on respect for authority' (Inglehart 1996, p. 661).

In the current climate it is likely that data used by Inglehart will be interpreted to show that the critical awareness targeted by those who worked for political education in the past has already been achieved. This may, according to Prime Minister Blair, have already gone too far. 'Duty', he says, 'is an essential Labour concept' (Blair 1995). As such, there is unlikely to be a revival of interest in explicit citizenship education in the near future, although of course there may well be a return to, or – more accurately – a continuation of, a form of implicit political education which stresses duty and does not require a formal programme of learning. The recent QCA report (QCA 1998) argues for a statutory entitlement without programmes of study. The above comment is, of course, made very tentatively. The present authors want something to happen and now seems to be a time when there are good reasons to be optimistic. Indeed, we are aware that making positive statements may contribute, if only in a very limited way, to action being taken. That said, we do not think that a professional development of citizenship education is by any means a foregone conclusion.

The Conceptual/Geographical Focal Point of Reform

During recent decades, characterizations of political education have been developed using geographical frameworks which are, in fact, a way of representing more substantial conceptual positions.

Prior to the 1970s, civic education was dominated by descriptions of some local but, more especially, national considerations. International contexts were not completely ignored and, for example, the League of Nations Union, the Council for Education in World Citizenship and the Parliamentary Group for World Government undertook very valuable work. However, the normal scenario involved the transmission of arcane information about, for example, traditions and procedures of the House of Commons. Political literacy did range far more widely and examples of international work for classrooms can easily be cited (Crick and Porter 1978), but both the personal and the international elements became much more strongly represented in the reforms of the 1980s.

From at least the 1980s, and rather distinct from the reforms associated with the new educations, has been the influence of Europe. This has been heightened dramatically in the 1980s and 1990s as national governments have responded to various European initiatives (Osler and Starkey 1996; Davies and Sobisch 1997; Convery et al. 1997; Evans et al. 1997). In England, however, Europe is often used at least partly as an arena for national development (de Beer 1997), and there is little that is taught directly to pupils about their new citizenship.

The global perspective has also reduced. While there are teachers who retain an internationalist position, models of citizenship which purport to look beyond the nation state seem to speak less to them than do other characterizations. In fact, teachers see citizenship as something which is given real expression mainly in local terms (Davies et al. 1997). This local expression is demonstrated in the face of strong pressure for teachers to emphasize national identity in attempts at cultural restorationism (Crawford 1996; Phillips 1997). While teachers reject the latter, the former could not be described as that which emerges from a radical perspective.

What do these shifts over the decades from national to personal/global to local mean? It seems that there has been a change from an approach which looked for cognitive understanding of political issues to an affective appreciation of what it means to strive for a better world to, currently, a concern for involvement in local issues (with perhaps some limited awareness of Europe) so that one can be seen as a good citizen. The definition of latter could be interpreted very negatively. There is the potential for young people's idealism to be exploited in a non-academic undifferentiated altruism. Whether, in the immediate future, the positive aspects of these developments are promoted remains to be seen, but at this point there seems little cause for optimism as the potentially quietist elements of political education seem more to the fore than other more ambitious features.

Ideologies and Intellectual Trends as the Motors of Reform

The period covered by this chapter largely encompasses various transitions, including those from the ideologies of the cold war, to the 'end of history', and to postmodernism.

Political literacy, with its high point in the 1970s, attracted critics from the political right and left in a way which must have been rather pleasing. To be criticized by both Tapper and Salter (1979) and by O'Keefe (1986) while being supported by HMI and the DES seems like skilful positioning. Research seemed to suggest that practice and the advice from LEAs showed a desire for 'teachers to present students with a balanced range of alternative positions on each issue' (Stradling 1987, p. 13). A moderate liberal framework was essential for success.

Global education, however, attempted a far more radical approach and failed. Projects became entangled in a web of accusation and counter-accusation, with little research being available to demonstrate that indoctrination was not being attempted. Lister has argued that charges of third worldism, one-sided disarmament and 'every country and culture but my own', were hard to rebut from those already identified with party politics and the promotion of substantive answers to single issues. Although there has probably never been a context in which debates about educational techniques have been informed by serious evaluative research, it is still not possible to avoid the conclusion that this aspect was particularly lacking from the development of 'new' educations.

There is some evidence of individuation in value positions (Hoelman and Ester 1994), and although postmodernism has been given intelligent expression in educational discussions (e.g. Gilbert 1995), it has failed. It has been characterized by negative fragmentation and has the potential for elitism (Appleby et al. 1994; Evans 1997). Very important is its failure to make any real inroads into teachers' thinking (Davies and Williams 1998).

However, the end of history thesis (Fukuyama 1992) has had far more success. This suggests, simply, that we are all now part of the same liberal capitalist world and that fundamental ideological struggle is at an end. This, though, is not necessarily to be welcomed by those wishing to promote political education. Rather, if teachers are continuing to promote what they feel can be described as common-sense and moderate rather than political points of view, opportunities for more searching and substantial political education may be missed. The indoctrination by the centre may continue.

Thus, unless they could be interpreted as being supportive of an existing mainstream position, the ideological shifts and intellectual trends of recent decades essentially seem to have had little long-term effect. There may have been radical positions taken in the 1980s but even they may have been less radical than the commentators of the new right believed, and in any case they did not succeed. Generally, there has been a continued consensual approach.

Implementation in Schools

The main way in which reforms associated with citizenship education have been driven has been subject to important changes. During the 1970s, a research and development project and the work of subject associations could be seen gathering important support from official national bodies.

During the 1980s, an interesting shift took place in what now seems to be the preparation of the ground for centralist intervention. Local education authorities were expected to develop curriculum guidelines for their schools. Since at least 1979, teachers have been used to some sort of active interference in the curriculum. The guidelines explicitly for political education, however, were relatively few and had little impact on teachers (Davies 1992). The Education Reform Act of 1988, which would deliberately exclude political education (Davies 1994a; 1994b), did have a major impact on restructuring schools. This was particularly so for pupils aged under 11, where subject teaching became much more important, and in humanities faculties in secondary schools where political issues had sometimes been taught. With the recent establishment of a working group under the chairmanship of Bernard Crick, we seem to have the working party of the 1970s together with the force of centralism of the 1980s and 1990s but lacking the detail of the curriculum changes associated with the latter time. The reform of the National Curriculum in the year 2000 will not be the same as its original development. Whether this will lead to radically different outcomes than those which have occurred in recent decades remains to be seen.

CONCLUSION

The last three decades have seen the emergence of an interest in political learning. Political literacy was overtaken by the new educations and currently there are debates about the nature of citizenship education. There have been valuable shifts from a narrow study of academic politics to issues which concern majorities.

The nature of the emergence of citizenship education has had more to do, however, with rhetoric from policy makers and project participants than with action by teachers and pupils in schools. The limited implementation that has occurred has been driven by a sense of crisis, and political education has ebbed during times of consensus and received widespread acceptance only when introduced in a way that is perceived to be non-threatening to notions of political stability. There is some cause for optimism with the recent report by Crick (QCA 1998), who, arguably, was part of the most successful incursion into political education during the period under review. QCA is caught in a number of dilemmas: the desire to make change without overburdening teachers; the need to develop civic engagement without promoting an agenda which could be criticized for having an undesirably narrow political focus which would lead to accusations of indoctrination; and the value of a broad-brush approach which recognizes the essential nature of morality, communities, identity and so very many other issues while also wishing to develop something which is intellectually coherent. We fervently hope that recent work will succeed: this book aims at assisting constructive developments. The work of the QCA committee is positive. But in aiming 'at no less than a change in the political culture of this country both nationally and locally' (QCA 1998, p. 4) the scale of the task must not be underestimated.

Part II
The Methods and Findings of the Research Project

2 Researching Teachers' Perceptions of Good Citizenship and Educational Provision

Conclusions based only on opinion and conjecture have little merit, particularly when speculation presumes to offer recommendations intended to affect change. There is arrogance in the assumption that intellectual theory alone should inform and influence educational practice. All too often conclusions based on what is termed 'research' have in reality sprung from well-meant but informal explorations of a topic. While the results of such examinations may well provide valuable information, the authors of this book are convinced that if analyses are to go beyond mere speculation, it is critically important to have in place a firm and scholarly foundation for conclusions reached or recommendations offered.

That 'firm and scholarly' foundation is provided by strong research methodology used in the comprehensive citizenship project from which the findings are drawn, and which is explained in some detail in this chapter. The variety of data resources used throughout considerably strengthens this research, designed to discover teacher's perceptions of the qualities and influences of citizenship and the subsequent analysis of the implications for educational practice. The simultaneous use of two sound research approaches in a single study – qualitative (i.e. one-to-one teacher interviews) and quantitative (i.e. statistically analysed questionnaire data) – adds much to the body of substantive research in this field. Such scientific research provides a data-based rationale for conclusions: better informing practice through empirical data and more subjective, qualitative analysis.

AN OVERVIEW OF THE RESEARCH

The Comprehensive Research Project

The research conducted in England, and which provides the foundation of this book, was part of a multi-nation study designed to learn more about citizenship education in various countries, teachers' perceptions of citizenship, and the implication of those perceptions for the classroom. The survey and interview questions utilised in the research were developed and refined as part of the comprehensive project initiated at Seattle Pacific University in the State of Washington in the United States. A total of six countries participated in the overall project; quantitative and qualitative analyses were *conducted separately* so results are clearly representative of each country. The intention and design of the research was that results were to be completely independent findings – findings most interesting for provocative dialogue at the project's end. The project was not designed nor intended to be comparative research. The focus of this volume, and all data presented and discussed, is only related to project research in England.

Finding out what teachers think provides a reasonable starting point for addressing a range of issues related to education for citizenship. The first and primary approach to the research study took the form of a questionnaire survey instrument designed to do just that (*the quantitative research component*). The major focus was on discovering teacher perceptions of the qualities of good citizenship. Related information about citizenship was derived from all sections of the two-sided survey form. Data obtained from the survey was assessed through statistical analyses. Subsequent interviews with primary and secondary teachers (*the qualitative research component*) added a second and rich layer to research findings. Structured teacher interviews allowed more thorough examination as teachers were asked to explore their personal and professional perceptions with regard to citizenship.

Upon compiling results from statistical analysis and interview data, researchers in England were able to characterize four clearly emerging concepts of citizenship, list teacher-identified qualities of a 'good' citizen, and discern teacher views regarding influences on and threats to a child's citizenship. Further, based on the survey instrument and interview research, a list was generated of what practical classroom applications teachers believe would help in developing a child's citizenship. Finally, when statistically comparing survey responses with the questionnaire's demographic section, then adding knowledge gained from the qualitative portion of the research, a picture emerged from which conclusions could reasonably be drawn, and informed questions posed related to this complex and significant issue.

The Research Questions

Four specific research questions were posed. Each was addressed by quantitative methods, qualitative methods, a review of existing literature, a historical overview, or a combination of some or all of these methods. Certainly, these research findings contribute to better understanding of citizenship in a wider context as part of the multi-nation study; however, the four research questions were designed to be specific to England. They deal with three dimensions of inquiry. The first dimension was to determine how congruent teacher perceptions are with the articulated intent and actual framework of the National Curriculum in England. The second dimension was designed to determine if perceptions tend to differ among teachers on the basis of their ethnicity, gender, age, the level taught and their professional training and experience. The third dimension involved assessing how well teacher perceptions reflect history and social development in England during the last century, including the relatively new experience of the European community.

Following are the research questions which guided the study, including a brief explanation of how each was addressed by the research methodology of the project.

Research Question 1

What are the qualities of good citizenship perceived by teachers in primary schools and secondary comprehensive schools in England?

This question was addressed primarily through quantitative data analysis based on teacher responses obtained from the survey. Analysis ranged from simple comparisons to more complex procedures, so the data could be examined in terms of the theoretical framework provided by examination of recent social and political history. Qualitative interview data added depth and dimension to the statistical analyses.

Research Question 2

Are teachers' perceptions of the qualities of good citizenship congruent with expressed principles and ideals of the National Curriculum in England?

This research question was primarily addressed through qualitative methods: in this case, one-to-one interviews. However, some statistical data, particularly the data related to emerging constructs, was particularly helpful in determining how congruent the perceptions appeared to be with the expressed realities of the actual mandated curriculum. An extensive review of literature, including the more recent history of the National Curriculum, was also instrumental in addressing the second research question.

Research Question 3

Do teachers' perceptions differ by sub-group?

This question was clearly assessed through statistical analysis comparing teacher responses on the survey to each of the six demographic subgroups of ethnicity, gender, age, level taught and professional training and experience. This is the single question in the study which is addressed only through quantitative methods. The other research questions were supported by some combination of quantitative and qualitative approaches, plus information and comparison based on a review of the literature.

Research Question 4

Do teachers' perceptions of good citizenship reflect a political view or a social/ humanitarian view of citizenship, and are elements of Euro-citizenship evident?

These were addressed both quantitatively and qualitatively. The four interesting constructs of citizenship which emerged from the more complex analysis provided a statistically generated framework by which teacher perceptions could be viewed from the perspective of social and political events in England. Qualitative data added much depth and detail, and specific examples to support the analysis of this research question.

THE QUANTITATIVE RESEARCH COMPONENT

Details of the Research Design

The quantitative component of the multi-nation study employed a descriptive survey research design in which the variables are clearly prespecified. This descriptive design was a concise, two-page survey instrument: a questionnaire comprising specific sections and questions. The instrument used for the quantitative portion of the project was the Citizenship Questionnaire (see Appendix, Citizenship Questionnaire) based on work done by Green (1987), Dynneson et al. (1987) and revised by Fouts (1995). Elements of the questionnaire used by these researchers were combined and modified by project team members, and new questions were added to fit the specific purposes of their research. Refinements were made to discover teacher perceptions of four clear dimensions related to concepts of citizenship. Specific items in each area were either developed by Green (1987), or were added by the multi-nation project researchers following additional literature review of theoretical models of citizenship (Riley 1996).

As part of the preparation involved in developing good foundational research design, the original version of the revised instrument was field tested early in 1995 with 40 teachers in the United States in order to check for clarity of understanding and clear terminology. Field testing is critical to see if potential overlapping of ideas or repetitions emerge which could ultimately misrepresent the results of statistical analysis. Following modifications, the questionnaire instrument was then administered to 201 elementary and secondary teachers from rural, urban and suburban schools to further establish construct validity and reliability.

The researchers working on the instrument agreed on the face validity; in other words, the questionnaire was clear and 'made sense' to teachers.

However, there was concern expressed about an apparent overlap of constructs and redundancy of specific items appearing in more than one of the six original areas. Following a statistical procedure termed 'principal components factor analysis with varimax rotation', only four of the six factors were found to have good construct validity. This resulted in two of the six areas being removed from the instrument.

The discussion above is for the purpose of introducing the reader to the overall research design of the multi-nation project and the origin of the survey and the interview questions applied to the comprehensive research study. For the purposes of this book, all explanation, analysis and discussion from this point on relates only to the research as it was conducted, implemented and analysed in England. That research – its implications and relevance – stands alone. The general framework of the questionnaire was much the same for each country participating in the comprehensive project. However, minor but appropriate revisions were made to the questionnaire that better reflected terminology common to each country (i.e. 'head teacher' rather than 'school principal', 'films' in place of 'movies'). In addition, after consulting with a limited sample of academics and teachers from England, the background information section was revised to reflect appropriate ethnic categories (official DfEE groups), and differing routes to teaching certificates (distinctly different than in the United States, China or any of the other participating countries). In England, this slightly revised Citizenship Questionnaire was termed Form AGB (i.e. First Form, Great Britain: see Appendix). While there was a similarity in the way initial data results were presented, literature review, demographic data, quantitative and qualitative analysis, applicability and subsequent discussion varied widely from country to country.

For the reader concerned that adequate research protocol was followed, and as a review of statistical analysis, the two-page questionnaire used in the study comprised five sections. Demographics, the first section, make up the six independent variables in the study. It appears at the beginning of the questionnaire and is designed to collect personal information from each teacher regarding ethnic group. In England, categories reflected the official Department for Education classifications: White, Black Caribbean, Black African, Black (other), Indian, Pakistani, Bangladeshi, Chinese, Asian (other), Other and Information Refused; gender (male or female); age (20–30, 31–40, 41–50, 51–60, over 60); route to professional training; and years of teaching experience.

Teachers certainly do not have a single common way of thinking any more than do other groups. Thus, information provided through the Demographics section, then statistically evaluated in conjunction with actual survey questions, prevents us from generalizing about what we believe 'all' teachers think. Instead, researchers can draw reasonable profiles of the population from whom those views are drawn which are helpful in interpreting survey data. For example, distinguishing between the views of experienced and inexperienced teachers, or older and younger teachers can lead to interesting speculations about where perceptions may have originated and how they appear to have effect in the classroom. Quantitative statistical analyses can help to provide this kind of information.

The remaining four sections of the instrument comprised four lead statements, each with a list of related indicators to which teachers were asked to indicate the strength of their agreement or disagreement. The general dependent variable for the most comprehensive and revealing statistics detailed in this chapter, and in which lay the foundation for the remaining analyses, is the first factor of the instrument – the section concerned with the qualities of a good citizen. Factor 'loadings' (a statistical procedure) for the qualities of good citizens ranged from 0.41 to 0.75, with alpha and split-half reliabilities of 0.84 and 0.88 respectively (Fouts 1995). This provides statistical support for the reliability of the 13 items, and subsequent use of the data that results from any statistical procedures.

The first section of the questionnaire (i.e. the instrument) consisted of a list of 13 behaviours or characteristics. The listing was headed by a statement: '*The following characteristics are qualities of a good citizen.*' Using a Likert-type scale, teachers were asked to respond to each statement. A Likert scale involves pinpointing one's views on a continuum in response to specific statements or questions. The 13 items in the first, key section of the four sections included:

- knowledge of current events
- participation in community or school affairs
- acceptance of an assigned responsibility
- concern for the welfare of others
- moral and ethical behaviour
- acceptance of authority of those in supervisory roles
- ability to question ideas
- ability to make wise decisions
- knowledge of government
- patriotism
- fulfilment of family responsibilities
- knowledge of world community
- tolerance of diversity within society.

For each statement, teachers were asked to demonstrate the strength of their agreement or disagreement that that quality characterized good citizenship. Responses were indicated by marking an 'x' on a continuous scale, with six choice categories ranging from 'SA' to indicate strong agreement that the item is representative of good citizenship to 'SD' indicating strong disagreement.

On the reverse of the form, identical categories were provided for the remaining three general dependent variables. These categories asked teachers to indicate factors they felt influenced their citizenship, factors they felt were a threat to the development of a child's citizenship, and finally, in an attempt to obtain practical information with direct implications for the curriculum, what might be done in the classroom which would be helpful in the development of a child's citizenship.

How the Quantitative Data was Obtained

Between 1995 and 1996, a number of teachers in England undertook the task of completing the citizenship survey instrument. Their time and effort in doing so provided the extensive data used in the statistical analyses discussed in this book. In determining schools where teachers were to be approached to complete the questionnaire, the aim was to create a sample which covered different geographical areas of England, drew from different areas (schools from metropolitan, urban and semi-urban locations were used), and which included both primary and secondary teachers. Each of the schools shared the sample foundational and core curriculum as required by the National Curriculum, as well as focusing, to varying degrees, on the cross-curricular components.

Teachers participating in the quantitative portion of the study were drawn primarily from the north and south of England, and from areas as diverse as North Yorkshire, Humberside, Cambridgeshire, Oxfordshire, Leicestershire and London. Research was first conducted among a sample of teachers in 11 secondary comprehensive state-maintained schools located in all these six geographic areas of England. A sample of 484 secondary school surveys was completed. Research then continued among a cross-section of teachers drawn from over 64 primary schools, resulting in an additional 195 questionnaires. A total of 679 teacher surveys thus forms the basis for the quantitative analysis.

To remain consistent with research designed to provide adequate representation of educational settings, this study was conducted in schools similar to those to which findings will be generalized. While all participating schools shared similar overall characteristics, there existed distinct environmental variations which are allowable in this type of research design (Borg and Gall 1989). Because school environments comprise unique communities reflecting a distinct school ethos, it is inappropriate to assume absolute similarity between schools. The sample, however, shared significant fundamental characteristics, as previously established, which allow findings to be appropriately generalized with some confidence.

Arranging and Conducting Data Collection: a Model

The secondary schools data (the sample from which data was collected first) may serve as a model for implementation during the actual data collection phase of any research project requiring extensive data collection. Early in 1995, schools were carefully identified with the assistance of university educators and authorities in citizenship studies. These individuals were initially approached because of their established standing in the area of citizenship education, or because of an expressed interest in the project and ongoing association with a substantial number of practising teachers.

Nine months prior to the data collection phase of the research, initial contact was made with schools to introduce the project and request participation. While schools were drawn from a range of socio-economic levels, each was similar in terms of diversity of students and the representative nature of that school to others in its geographic area. The sample included subgroups of teacher age, gender, ethnic group, professional teacher training, and years of teacher experience. In terms of the planned statistical analyses, a larger sample was utilized so that persons having different attributes in terms of the subgroups would be satisfactorily represented.

Six months prior to the planned data collection, head teachers of identified secondary schools received a detailed letter to further explain the study. The letter, which included a draft copy of the instrument, thanked them for their interest and outlined necessary requirements and time commitment. Specific suggestions were made regarding dates for an autumn visit in order personally to conduct the research with teachers. The agreement to participate rested in the hands of the teachers. In most cases, teaching staff were asked directly by the administrator if they were interested in participating. Formal agreement was only granted after teachers had been queried and positive responses obtained. The majority of representative schools were confirmed five months prior to the actual data collection.

When conducting a large-scale project, the co-ordination of organizational details takes much time and effort. It is, however, that organizational effort that translates a well-designed research idea into a practical, well-executed study yielding useful data – which is, after all, the point of the exercise. Prior to the actual data collection, significant communication took place with each of the eleven schools in order to finalize arrangements for administering the instrument in specially arranged or regularly scheduled staff meetings. Working within a research timeframe of three working weeks, it was necessary to organize meeting times convenient for each teaching staff. Additional considerations involved arranging meetings which fitted into each school's schedule, taking into account different regional term breaks, and organizing the research to allow the investigator adequate travel time within those six, often distant, geographic locations.

Prearranged visits to the secondary schools continued for three weeks of specific, on-site research. Data collection entailed personal visits to the majority of participating schools to explain, administer and collect the surveys. In most instances, teachers were assembled for a prearranged staff meeting – either a routine meeting, or one scheduled solely for the purpose of this research. A block of time ranging from 15 minutes to an hour was allotted, allowing adequate time for introductory comments about the multi-nation research study, instructions regarding the form and to thank teachers for their participation in the project.

The importance of completing both sections of the Citizenship Question-naire was emphasized. This better ensured completion of the background-demographic section and the continuous scale questions regarding perceptions of citizenship. To ensure a greater return rate, teachers were asked to respond to the questionnaire upon distribution, with all forms returned prior to the researcher's departure. In every observed instance, teachers appeared to give their full attention to the survey. It took an average of 7 to 14 minutes for participants to complete both sections. In the majority of schools, the head teacher or an assigned contact teacher facilitated distri-bution and collection of the instrument.

Teaching staff in each of the 11 participating secondary schools ranged in size from 50 to over a hundred teachers. Teachers from all subject areas participated by completing the survey instrument. This was highly desirable since the National Curriculum designed citizenship as a cross-curricular theme to permeate the curriculum across subject-matter lines. How this is accomplished in each classroom is highly dependent upon the individual teacher, and remains a matter of much discussion.

Based on teacher comment made early in the data collection – 'Exactly what do you mean by citizenship?' – it seemed prudent to make a special effort to emphasize at subsequent schools that it was not the intention to impose any definition. Rather, teachers were to approach statements contained in the survey from the perspective of their own understanding of the meaning of citizenship. Following this explanation, which was modelled at each site, teachers accepted 'I am interested in what you think' at face value, and no further concerns regarding the meaning of citizenship were expressed at remaining schools.

Extensive effort was made to organize data carefully the same day it was collected. Each returned and completed questionnaire was stamped with a note of the date and the school code. As every school is required to have available on request a detailed prospectus, outlining such specifics as number of pupils, teaching staff, curriculum, activities and school vision, such site-specific demographic information was also collected. Time with teachers and examination of the school prospectus provided researchers with a sense of the school community and school ethos.

Quantitative Data Analysis Procedures

Data obtained from the Citizenship Questionnaire was analysed in several ways. The statistical computer program 'SPSS' was used for data entry and analysis. During the data entry stage, an assistant aided in the process to verify the accuracy of each entry from the 484 Citizenship Questionnaire forms completed by teachers. For the first section, 'The following characteristics are important qualities of a good citizen', item means were computed and then rank ordered to provide a generic description of the total sample's view of the characteristics of a good citizen.

A second procedure was used to analyse the entire set of sample responses on the initial 13 items, employing a principal components factor analysis with varimax rotation – a complex procedure designed to identify related concepts. This procedure was selected in order to determine maximum variance between factors, and to discover what constructs might emerge from the data. Clear concepts did indeed emerge. It is these concepts or constructs that provide the most in-depth framework utilized for any remaining analysis. Upon emergence of comprehensible factors, mean scores were computed on each factor for each of the six subgroups. For those with an interest in the specific procedures utilized, rank orderings of the various subgroups and group differences on the factors scores were then compared using a one of two procedures: either a Mann Whitney-U procedure or the Kruskall–Wallis One-Way ANOVA procedure.

The Citizenship Questionnaire instrument comprising these five sections yielded all the quantitative statistical data used by the authors of this book in the examination of teachers' perceptions of citizenship and the implications of those perceptions for the curriculum. The most detailed analysis yielded came from the concepts arising from teacher-identified characteristics of the qualities of a good citizen, for these concepts inform the remainder of the data interpretation.

Four highly distinct concepts of citizenship clearly emerged from quantitative analysis of teacher responses. The data grouped qualities into meaningful constructs identified as the *informed* citizen, the *socially aware* citizen, the *dutiful* citizen and the *active* citizen. Specific qualities of fundamental importance were clearly identified by teachers in this study. These characteristics are most strongly associated with the construct of the socially aware citizen, including the attitudes and behaviours which reflect qualities of concern, moral and ethical behaviour and tolerance.

Useful data emerging from the remaining three sections provide a good picture of the percentage and frequency of teacher choices, with rank ordering of responses demonstrating clear priorities. Correlating this data with the wealth of qualitative information emerging from teacher interviews provides strong, research-based data to support the discussion, analyses, conclusions and recommendations discussed in this examination of citizenship education.

THE QUALITATIVE RESEARCH COMPONENT: INTERVIEWS

Details of the Research Design

The next step in the research project was to conduct individual interviews, geared towards obtaining more explicit information about what teachers believe about citizenship and citizenship education, and their own role in the process. Interviews commenced after the quantitative data had been collected from both primary and secondary schools and, for the most part, involved a different set of teachers. Two researchers worked together to set up interviews by sending a personal letter followed by a phone call. Respondents were told what the interview would be about, and assured of confidentiality. A careful 'set-up' process was used so that a range of teachers would be represented (i.e. primary and secondary, different subject areas, all within one geographical area in the north of England).

Qualitative research is a time-consuming process. Discounting the time needed to organize a schedule of interviews, researchers are engaged with respondents for a specified time and then must transcribe notes or recordings prior to commencing analysis. However, the depth of resulting information makes the effort well worth the time invested for researcher and respondent alike. In this case, 40 teachers from five primary schools and five secondary schools were interviewed, using the agreed schedule of questions used by all participants in the multi-nation project.

Citizenship interviews lasted between 30 and 90 minutes, with the average time approximately 35 minutes. Interviews were conducted privately, where distractions would be limited. Each interview began with a restatement of the purpose of the interview, a promise of confidentiality and a reassurance that there were no right or wrong answers, and that the interviewers truly 'wanted to know what they thought'. Interviewees were first asked to provide informally a brief sketch of themselves (i.e. professional background, teaching subject area any biographical information they chose to share). Then the standard questioning began.

Interview Question 1

Question 1 asked teachers what comes to mind when hearing the word 'citizenship'.

Researchers provided prompts such as 'What characteristics (or words to describe) do you think of?' A range of probes were used, including legal status, value of action, context of action (i.e. local, national), can a person be a citizen if they merely think and do not act, aspects of citizenship (i.e. political, economic).

Interview Question 2

Question 2 related to good citizenship in the context of schools.

Principally, researchers wanted to know if the understanding of citizenship teachers talked about in answer to the first question was the same as that which they would use in schools. Related to this were probes such as – 'When you think of a pupil as being a 'good citizen' of the school, what do you mean?' 'Why do you so describe them?' 'Why are the characteristics they possess so important?' 'Do you make any distinction between being a good citizen of the school and in the wider adult society?' 'How can we encourage good citizenship?' Discussion might commence around themes related to subject work, school ethos, behaviour, certification for citizenship activities or the value of voluntary work in the community.

Interview Question 3

Question 3 asked teachers if they would describe themselves as good citizens.

Teachers were encouraged to share the ways in which they believed they were good citizens, and share what influences they felt had been significant in the development of those qualities. Gentle probing related to family, religion, community and attitudes towards law helped them examine how they may have developed or acquired those characteristics.

Interview Question 4

Question 4 asked teachers how they believe they are rewarded or reinforced for being a good citizen – (if at all).

Teachers were asked to reflect on why they are good citizens and to assess how they are rewarded in school or in life for displaying those qualities. Probes related to asking them to think about who or what in the society or culture causes them to want to be a good citizen (i.e. family? reward system? fear of sanction?).

Finally, at the close of the interview, teachers were asked if they wanted to share anything else they had not been given the opportunity to mention. Teachers were then thanked for their personal time and professional contribution to the project.

The analysis of the interview materials falls into three clear 'characteristics' categories, which will be merely introduced here but explored in some depth in subsequent chapters. *Social concern characteristics* included a clear moral context, tolerance for a diversity of views and a clear sense of community; *knowledge characteristics* are highlighted as knowledge of political issues within citizenship discourse and of structures and political thinking; and *conservative characteristics* basically refers to a sense of patriotism and an acceptance of assigned responsibilities and authority. The analysis of the 'characteristic categories' confirms quantitative data and provides rich and detailed anecdotal support for these findings.

CONCLUSION

Specific research findings emerging from the quantitative research plus qualitative interview findings will appear in table and text form in Chapter 4 as part of the discussion regarding teachers' perceptions of key influences on the development of good citizenship. Subsequent findings will be detailed in Chapter 5, which will present data emerging from the questionnaire and interview research to support practical implications affecting practice.

When supported by a comprehensive literature review, it is a combination of statistical analysis, emerging constructs, interviews and subsequent comparisons which provide a sound basis from which to examine teacher perceptions with confidence, and inform discussion related to curricular implications with the same confidence. When well designed and implemented, a combination of quantitative and qualitative research methods provides the strongest possible foundation from which to proceed with confidence in the examination and improvement of citizenship education – indeed, to examine a topic within any context.

3 What Do Teachers Mean by Good Citizenship?

This chapter discusses teacher perceptions on what constitutes being a good citizen. It will fall into three main parts: a very brief recapitulation of methodological considerations, an account of questionnaire findings relevant to teacher perceptions on what constitutes good citizenship, and a much more substantial section highlighting the findings of the interview data. The quantitative and qualitative data convincingly reflect each other.

Put very briefly, our data strongly suggests that for our teachers good citizens are identified as individuals who have a high level of concern for the welfare of others, who conduct themselves in a strongly moral and ethical manner, who are very conscious of their community obligations, and who participate in the community within which they live. They characteristically bring to their dealings with others both tolerance of others' opinions and views and an acceptance of diversity within society. Among primary school teachers there is little evidence of citizenship as directed to the political sphere. There is some evidence among secondary school teachers of citizenship as bearing upon matters of a more ostensibly political nature. But common to all our teachers is the sense that good citizenship is primarily about meeting the obligations we stand under towards fellow members of a community.

SOME BRIEF METHODOLOGICAL COMMENTS

Both quantitative and qualitative data were collected from teachers in England. As mentioned in Chapter 2, a total of 679 teachers completed the questionnaire. The teachers were drawn from over 64 primary schools (195 questionnaires) and 11 secondary schools (484 questionnaires). Forty teachers from five primary schools and five secondary schools were interviewed, using the agreed schedule.

The aim was to create a sample which reflected the following criteria:

- a coverage of different geographical areas of England; schools from the north and south of England were used
- a distribution of different catchment areas; schools from metropolitan, urban and semi-urban locations were used
- inclusion of both primary and secondary schools. Primary schools cater largely for pupils aged 5–11 (although there is some variation with a few 4–11, 7–11 and 3–11 being used). Secondary schools largely cater for pupils aged 11–18, although again there was some variation with a few 11–16 schools being used. Given the smaller populations of primary schools, far more primary schools had to be included in the sample than secondary schools.

The interviews were conducted by two researchers. A range of teachers across both the primary and secondary phases, and across different curriculum areas, were interviewed. All teachers who supplied interview data came from within one geographical area of the north of England.

QUESTIONNAIRE FINDINGS

Respondents were asked to assess on the scale 1–6 the measure of their agreement or disagreement with the schedule of items listing possible important characteristics of a good citizen. Strong agreement was represented by 6 through to strong disagreement represented by 1. A mean score of 3.5 or greater is interpreted as an overall positive view of a given characteristic and a mean score of less than 3.5 is indicative of an overall negative attitude to a characteristic.

The calculated rank order by means of each of the items offered as constitutive of being a good citizen corresponds very closely with the combined percentages strongly agreeing with the statement (see Table 3.1). Analysis of the data lent itself to three clear categories with the following members:

1 *Social concern characteristics* Concern for the welfare of others, moral and ethical behaviour and tolerance of diversity within society, and
2 *Knowledge characteristics* Knowledge of government, knowledge of current events, knowledge of world community, ability to question ideas, and
3 *Conservative or subject/obedient role characteristics* Acceptance of the authority of those in a supervisory role, patriotism, acceptance of assigned responsibilities.

The mean factor scores for *each teacher* were calculated by averaging the responses to each of the questions on the individual factors. The factor mean score is to be interpreted in the same way as the item means. The factor

Table 3.1 Rank order by means of total sample on the qualities of good citizenship

| | | | Combined responses[a] | |
Variable	M	SD	f	%
Concern	5.62	0.63	635	93.5
Moral	5.49	0.77	609	89.7
Tolerance	5.39	0.85	585	86.2
Fulfilment	5.12	1.06	519	76.4
Ability	4.88	1.01	454	66.9
Make wise decisions	4.84	1.08	459	67.6
Acceptance	4.63	1.17	395	58.1
Participation	4.58	0.97	376	55.3
Authority	4.52	1.16	384	56.6
Knowledge	4.48	1.08	340	50.1
World	4.24	1.08	279	41.1
Government	3.87	1.17	196	28.8
Patriotism	2.97	1.36	83	12.2

a 'Combined responses' columns report combined frequency and percentage of respondents selecting choices 1 or 2. Of six possible choices, selection of '1' indicates 'strong agreement' with the item.

means are shown in Table 3.2. The 13 items pertaining to characteristics of good citizenship were analysed to identify distinct factors. Three factors emerged from the final rotated solution using both principal components and principal factor analyses with varimax rotation. Three items which loaded on more than one factor were eliminated (see Table 3.3).

Table 3.2 Factor scores and rank order for the entire sample of teachers for the 13 qualities of good citizenship

Factors	Item X
Social concern characteristics	5.5
Knowledge characteristics	4.4
Conservative characteristics	4.0

Overall, these data indicate that social concern characteristics are seen as more important in the characterization of a good citizen than the other factors.

Detailed examination of the frequency distribution of these mean scores reveals:

- 542 (about 80 per cent) of the total sample of teachers rated social concern characteristics more important than other factors.

Table 3.3 Factor and item loadings for the 13 qualities of good citizenship

Item	Factor loading
Factor 1: Knowledge characteristics	
Knowledge of government	0.81
Knowledge of current events	0.78
Knowledge of world community	0.78
Ability to question ideas	0.66
Factor 2: Social concern characteristics	
Concern for the welfare of others	0.80
Moral and ethical behaviour	0.73
Tolerance of diversity within society	0.59
Factor 3: Conservative characteristics	
Acceptance of authority	0.77
Patriotism	0.75
Acceptance of an assigned responsibility	0.51

- 28 (about 4 per cent) of the teachers rated the knowledge characteristics as more important in a good citizen than social concern or conservative characteristics.
- 15 (about 2 per cent) of the teachers rated conservative characteristics as more important to a good citizen than the social concern and knowledge characteristics. (This does not add up to 100 per cent as some teachers rated two or more factors as equally important.)

Further, 69 teachers (about 11 per cent) had a negative attitude (below 3.5) towards conservative characteristics, while 30 teachers (about 4 per cent) had a negative attitude towards the knowledge characteristics and just one teacher had a negative attitude to social concern characteristics.

What seems plain enough in the light of the foregoing is that the teachers represented by the questionnaire data very strongly identify with an idea of a good citizen finding expression in an active concern for the welfare of others. Both in terms of mean rankings of items offered as important qualities of a good citizen and the mean rankings of the factors, it is plain that concern for the welfare of others, moral and ethical behaviour, and tolerance of diversity of behaviour comfortably occupy the three leading positions in the rank ordering. It seems that foremost in the minds of those responding to the questionnaire is a notion of good citizenship characterized by a recognition of the importance of the obligations and responsibilities we owe others with whom we spend our lives.

It seems equally clear that while respondents typically agree that knowledge and conservative characteristics are overall important elements in the make-up of the good citizen, relatively they are significantly less important than an active concern for the welfare of others. And that in the composite image emerging from the questionnaire data, knowledge characteristics score more highly than conservative characteristics as constitutive of what it is to be a good citizen. This picture may be distorted, however, by the extremely negative attitude revealed through the questionnaire towards 'patriotism' as an element in the make-up of a good citizen. The little interview data there is of attitudes towards patriotism suggests that it is identified with what is viewed as disagreeable, because jingoistic, manifestations of 'my country, first and last'.

THE INTERVIEWS

We asked all teachers the following questions:

- When you hear the word citizenship, what comes to mind? What characteristics (or words to describe) do you think of?
- When you think of a pupil as being a 'good citizen' of the school, what do you mean? Why do you so describe them? Why are the characteristics they possess so important? Do you make any distinction between being a good citizen of the school and in the wider adult society?
- Would you describe yourself as a good citizen? If so, in what ways? If not, why not? Who importantly influenced you in your growth to being a good citizen?
- Why are you a good citizen? Are you rewarded in any way for being a good citizen?

The analysis of the interview materials revealed the same patterns as found in the questionnaire data. A close and sustained reading of teacher comments generated the same set of categories as had emerged from the quantitative data: social concern characteristics; conservative characteristics; knowledge characteristics. All of our data is presented and structured around these categories.

Social Concern Characteristics

The following key themes emerged from the analysis of the data: good citizenship as a matter of meeting community obligations; citizenship as more a matter of morality than of law; tolerance of diversity of views as key to being a good citizen; the importance and nature of participation as the mark of a good citizen.

Good Citizenship as Meeting Community Obligations

Our analysis of the interview data is very much of a piece with the questionnaire findings. The teachers we spoke to characteristically associated being a good citizen with meeting the responsibilities owed to others as fellow members of the community.

> My understanding of being a citizen is that you look after other people and you help other people and we're supportive, being a supportive community.

> We all have different backgrounds, we all have different talents and it's a good citizen who uses whatever talent he or she has for the benefit of the community.

There is no doubt that community as found in teacher responses is preponderantly locally conceived. There is evidence that some teachers are conscious of the tendency to extend the notion of citizenship, and its associated responsibilities, to the more global conceptions presently emerging on the back of the growth of this country's membership of the European Union, the Human Rights movement, the increasing interdependence of countries and economies, and world-wide anxieties about the future of the environment. The following quotation, while atypical, is a striking example of this awareness.

> The two elements of citizenship in my life are responsibilities to other people and responsibilities to the planet. . . . It used to be adequate to be a good citizen in your community. Because your community embraced the means of production of all the artefacts you used and the means of production for all the food that you used and they completely stratified a society. Nowadays that's no longer adequate. We rely upon people assembling our washing machines in Korea. There's so much of what we use and what comes into our lives that is miles away that it requires much more education nowadays to be a good citizen than it used to.

But the above sentiment *was* unusual and it was more common to find teachers exemplifying discharging responsibilities as a good citizen in terms of parking the car properly, not letting the dog bark too loudly, picking up paper litter, etc., and the contrast then being made with those behaviours that are careless of other people's property and interests, e.g. vandalism in all of its manifestations – the latter being seen as definitive of what it is not to be a good citizen. The rationale for the kinds of behaviour noted and approved of was that such behaviour is indicative and revealing of the fact 'that everyone has a responsibility to keep the community functioning'. It is inevitably a feature of the behaviours mentioned that they involve agents in immediate contact with those around them – as neighbours. It was remarked that even if the idea of citizenship was extended beyond 'the local' to embrace the national, the international, the global, nevertheless the ideal of being a good citizen, rather like charity, started at home. Even the most ambitious hopes for being good citizens of the world were premised on the idea that

> most people become good citizens of their local community and then they are empowered to start looking wider.

But with some significant exceptions (mainly secondary school teachers), talk of good citizenship was largely parochial. We mean by 'parochial' that a good citizen was conceptualized largely in terms of the community and society within which individuals passed their lives.

Citizenship as a Matter of Morality

Time and time again, respondents, while recognizing that being a citizen was partly a matter of legal status, affirmed that it was the moral dimensions of citizenship that mattered to them. This is a typical comment:

> So certainly I would see the legal aspects of citizenship but that doesn't particularly interest me. I see it more as a moral issue than a legal one.

In keeping with the implications of the moral dimensions of good citizenship, a distinction was occasionally drawn between the bad citizen who acts in ways contrary to the interests of other individuals and the larger community, the good citizen who is conscious of the interests of others and the wider society and acts accordingly, and the passive citizen who is best characterized as someone who speaks the language of good citizenship but who does nothing positive by way of action to further the interests of others or the common good. Time and time again the language of caring, unselfishness, co-operation and demonstrating respect is used to give substance to the distinguishing characteristics of the good citizen, be the context school or the wider community.

Reinforcing such sentiments are those remarks to be found in the interview materials suggesting that one of the casualties of the Thatcher years was precisely that regard for others so many respondents laid so much emphasis upon. Thus:

> I don't think Thatcher's Britain had encouraged people to become good citizens so to speak because it was always put yourself first, wasn't it?

Toleration of a Diversity of Views

Given the heavy emphasis in almost all the replies – primary or secondary – on the ethical/moral dimension of good citizenship, it should occasion little surprise that tolerance of diversity of views, values, opinions and those not like themselves, figures as constitutive of the good citizen. Teachers often referred to the significance of the tolerance of other views and value systems. The following quotation captures nicely the gist of this sentiment:

> For my value system to be accepted even if it is not the same as somebody else's and equally I should accept theirs. I think that kind of tolerance is what being a good citizen is about. In terms of the community functioning effectively, if you don't have that tolerance base, it can't work.

A primary school teacher reiterates the thrust of the above in her observations about a good citizen in the school context when she says of such pupils:

> They're very fair. Very fair in the way they treat friends and even people that aren't their friends. They seem to recognize that there are people who are not quite the same as them. Some children are quite mean, they haven't yet realized that you can't go through life being mean to people who are different to you. And the ones that stand out are fair minded and live and let live. And they try and include different people . . . they know it's not acceptable to leave somebody out because they are not as bright as them, who might not particularly be in the same group as that person but they'll just get on with it.

The Importance of Participation

Only 10.8 per cent of teachers had a negative view of participation in community and school affairs as an important characteristic of the good citizen. In a context in which a sense of obligation to the community was paramount it is, perhaps, not surprising that the notion of participation in the community emerged as a key theme in discussion on how one discharged the responsibilities of being a good citizen. Participation embraces the idea of individual attachment to a cause advancing some collective goal of the local community to which one belongs. It was not uncommon to find remarks such as the following in response to the (rather invidious) questions as to whether they were good citizens:

> In terms of being a good citizen I try to get very involved with the three villages served by our diocese . . . I would hope that by getting involved I'm a good citizen.

> It's about somebody who participates . . . you can't sit at home and think nice thoughts . . . You've actually got in some form to be seen to be contributing and playing your part I think in the way our society develops and runs itself.

And those who doubted if they were as good a citizen as they would like to be expressed their anxieties in terms of not having the energy after a hard day's teaching to get involved (participate) in their community's activities.

> The biggest reason I don't feel that I am a good citizen is that I don't feel as though I have the time and energy to be one, which is an awful thing to say.

> I know there are things that I don't do that I should do and one thing is that I'm really too busy to be socially concerned with the outside world.

Again, for a minority, there was a wish to extend the notion of participation beyond their immediate environment. For those operating with a more generous conception of citizenship – embracing European or even world citizenship – participation also involved belonging to organizations such as Amnesty, Christian Aid, Greenpeace or Charter 88.

It is worth remarking at this stage that the emphasis upon participation within a community expressing itself in voluntary action does not, as far as our teachers go, indicate any ideological commitment to the idea that the role of the state in our lives should be cut back. In this respect, the sentiment is opposed to that which informed the encouragement of voluntary action during the Thatcher years in Britain. Being a good citizen is an expression of our obligations and responsibilities towards others for their own sake, because that is how we *should* behave one towards the other.

The reference to communities within which lives are passed, the talk of participation subsuming as it does local causes and concerns through to the less parochial concerns of human rights, world poverty and the like, the emphasis upon co-operation as an aspect of good citizenship, the fundamental insistence upon the pursuit of the common good, the interests of the wider society – all these locate the concept of being a good citizen and taking action consonant with good citizenship firmly within the social domain. In short, there is more to being a citizen than satisfying the requirements of personal morality. The notion of being a good citizen reflects more than a commitment to an undifferentiated altruism.

Conservative Characteristics

Acceptance of Authority

We made the (we hope) reasonable assumption that references in interviews to the importance of being law abiding, following an institution's (in this case, typically the school's) rules, might plausibly be used as evidence of a recognition of the importance of authority in human affairs.

A negative view of acceptance of authority of those in a supervisory role was held by 16.2 per cent of teachers. However, there are many references to the need to keep the rules. It is fairly common for teachers in response to the question whether they are good citizens to cite their own characteristic obedience to the laws of the land as evidence of being good citizens.

> On a very basic level I would say, yes, I was a good citizen because I don't destroy things. I obey the laws.

Teachers, in part, anyway, define good citizens of the school in terms of their acceptance of school rules.

> First of all they keep the rules, don't they? You know, and they don't do anything that really causes problems.

But there is not any celebration of being law abiding and rule following for their own sake. All the references to law following are invariably qualified by how it is laws promote social harmony and the avoidance of social chaos.

> I don't break the rules that are there for the smooth running of society.

> if you, like, obey the rules and do it for the good of everyone else and understand the reasons underlying it.

A theme occasionally picked up in connection with the operation of the law in our lives is that while social harmony is important, it is not so important that being a good citizen is just to be identified with following the law. On occasion, it might be the mark of a good citizen that they set their face against the demands of the law:

> Yes, there are occasions where you can be a good citizen by doing exactly the opposite of what the law demands [this in respect of poll tax legislation].

> And I think sometimes we think we're a good citizen by being peaceful and pacifying and keeping it all smooth and it's not. I think sometimes

> it's [being] a good citizen to cause ripples . . . and I think sometimes a good citizen is one who rebels against authority.

The sense of law and rules as properly subject to critical scrutiny is very much of a piece with the evidence from our research suggesting that schools certainly see as part of their task, in the encouragement of a good citizenry, the ability to ask questions. One respondent struck a reconciling stance on this matter by asserting the possibility that the good citizen will go against the law while, at the same time, affirming the very high likelihood that,

> on the other hand, I think that in 99 per cent of cases they really do come down to the same thing where the law in most practical cases [does coincide with the] ordinary basic moral values assumed by the community.

Acceptance of Assigned Responsibilities

There is some lack of clarity in the responses of teachers in this area. Only 14.2 per cent of teachers had a negative view (a marking of 3 or below) of acceptance of assigned responsibilities as a characteristic of the good citizen. However, it is difficult from our interview data to hazard a guess as to what was understood by questionnaire respondents when they made this judgement on the relative importance of this category.

Patriotism

The idea of patriotism, however interpreted, does not figure very prominently in the interview data. At the conceptual level, patriotism suffers from a crucial ambiguity between being a love of one's country because of the values, sentiments and principles for which it stands – which may well recommend themselves to a critical moral consciousness – and the idea of 'my country first and last'. The former, we suggest, is respectable; the latter 'the last refuge of the scoundrel'. The only two references to patriotism seemed informed by more of the latter interpretation:

> I abhor all the kind of flag waving, national anthems, monarchy, all that kind of thing.

> I shy away from anything that has connotations of flags and countries and nationalism.

We strongly suspect that the strongly negative view taken of patriotism, as revealed in the questionnaire findings – it was the lowest ranked of all the possible characteristics of the good citizen and the one with the highest negative attitude towards it – reflects the equally negative connotations of patriotism given expression in the quotes just given.

Knowledge Characteristics

There are two main issues which are highlighted by teacher responses: knowledge of political issues within citizenship discourse; knowledge of structures and critical thinking.

It is worth noting initially that it is in respect of knowledge characteristics that our interview data revealed the greatest difference between primary school teachers and secondary teachers. The accounts offered of citizenship by secondary school teachers drew very much more on the discourse of political and civil rights and responsibilities than did those of primary teachers. There is much more on the importance of encouraging and participating in the democratic process. Why this should be so is a matter for further investigation. It might just be the case that the secondary teachers interviewed were in some way idiosyncratic by virtue of the subjects they teach – an over-representation of history, social science teachers, teachers with responsibilities for personal and social education and so on. It might be that having responsibility for those nearer to the world of work and the possible exercise of their democratic rights engenders a heightened awareness of such issues.

Knowledge of Political Issues within Citizenship Discourse

It was in relation to knowledge about wider systems and conceptual awareness that the differences between primary and secondary teachers seemed clearest. There is a much greater sensitivity to the dimension of issues of citizenship by the secondary teachers. There is a greater readiness to associate citizenship with the enjoyment of political, social and economic rights.

> I think automatically of political rights . . . freedom of speech, freedom of press and political participation through elections, debating and so on, participation within a political party . . . I think of political liberty, the political freedom aspect of it more than anything else.

> Well, for me, it's understanding democratic processes and the importance of them . . . generally, I think it's to do with the way democracy and politics works.

This ostensibly political dimension to matters of citizenship is reflected in the kinds of issues broached under the guise of citizenship education. Issues to do with racism, sexism, embracing one's democratic responsibilities, recognizing the democratic rights of others, encouragement of an awareness of national and international issues, the importance of human rights concerns, the significance of parliamentary democracy and the like, are suggested as part of a school curriculum recognizing an obligation to prepare young people to be citizens in their community. There is a larger commitment to 'encouraging them [i.e. the students] to be more politically aware'. It is, perhaps, predictable that the more generous conception of citizenship going beyond the immediacy of the local community is more in evidence among our secondary school teachers. It is, perhaps, predictable that references to membership of Amnesty, Greenpeace, Christian Aid, Action Aid, Charter 88 and so on pepper this batch of teacher responses.

Of the 20 interview responses from primary school teachers, however, only one quite specifically mentions

> [the] political side of things. Franchise, having the vote, elections and so on. Freedom of thought, freedom of speech, the right to work for change too.

References to community beyond the immediate locality, to the more overtly political overtones of citizenship discourse, to pressure groups of various kinds serving human rights concerns are notably absent in the responses of the primary school teachers interviewed in this segment of the research. But, again, common to all responses, irrespective of whether they are from the secondary or primary school sector, is the emphasis upon the good citizen being one who is concerned about and seeks to advance the interests of others and the wider society (appropriately defined). In this respect, the more politicized responses of the secondary school teachers on citizenship issues more generally do not make much difference. The context may be more generously drawn, but there is no very real evidence to support a belief that a good citizen is distinguished for the secondary teachers of our sample by their greater participation in the processes associated with the operation of a mature democracy. It still seems to be a matter of doing good, advancing causes because individuals care for other individuals, either singly or collectively. To that extent, the outstanding social concern orientation is untouched by anything said by the secondary school teachers.

Knowledge of Structures and Critical Thinking

Some teachers drew attention to the importance of relevant knowledge:

> Becoming aware of the structures of society, the political structures . . . and that these things are essential for a healthy society and that they need to be aware of these structures and to participate in society they need to be fully aware.

> Awareness of how systems operate means that if you wish to progress, you operate within these frameworks.

There was nothing to suggest that teachers favoured a simplistic return to an old-fashioned approach of teaching the British Constitution. Teachers were very keen to emphasize that the knowledge had to be used as an aid to critical thinking rather than merely be received. In fact, the questionnaire data showed a less than wholehearted support of knowledge *per se*. The percentage of the teachers who had a negative view of knowledge of government as a characteristic of a good citizen was 32.4; 20.7 per cent of teachers had a negative view of knowledge of world community as an important characteristic of a good citizen; and 14.5 per cent did not think that knowledge of current events was important to being a good citizen. The interview data emphasized the need for critical thinking as opposed to the acceptance of information in bringing students to appreciate

> how important it is for them to make up their own minds and to think about things.

The attitudes towards these intellectual and moral virtues which were discussed by teachers as being vital elements of good citizenship were of two kinds: either as good in themselves or (and for our purposes more significantly and importantly) as goods, the possession of which helps in the achievement of goals. We suggest that the ability to question, and the possession of relevant knowledge are best understood within the context of a concern for good citizenship as instrumental goods. Lacking relevant knowledge, the ability to advance the wellbeing of others is greatly diminished. Without a commitment to the furtherance of these goods, the ambitions encapsulated in the good citizen ideal of advancing the welfare of others are unlikely to be realized.

CONCLUSION

The primary emphasis in this chapter has been on teacher perceptions of the characteristics associated with being a good citizen. In our terminology, what is revealed is the overwhelming consensus informing both the quantitative and qualitative data that a good citizen is someone who exhibits social concern characteristics, a primary concern for the welfare of others, a preparedness to be tolerant of others, their opinions, sentiments and general outlooks, a disposition towards moral behaviour and places great emphasis upon the importance of participation within the community (QCA 1998, p. 14). There is some evidence that the secondary school teachers in our sample conceive of the community within which good citizenship is to be exhibited more globally than do our primary school teachers. Talk of being a citizen of Europe or of the world is more in evidence. But irrespective of the scope of community, the good citizen looks beyond his or her own concerns with a view to advancing the welfare of those others. There is evidence from our interview data that our secondary school teachers conceive of citizenship in terms of enjoying certain political, civil and economic rights, and that the proper task of citizenship education is to bring students to an awareness of those rights.

4 Teacher Perceptions of the Key Influences upon the Development of Good Citizenship

This chapter explores how teachers perceive the development of their own citizenship, examines factors they determine to have been most instrumental as it evolved, and ascertains their perception of contemporary threats to the development of good citizenship among their students. Given the broad characterization of citizenship with which teachers work, perhaps one way to get at the essence of how to address successfully citizenship education is to deepen the scope of exploring their perceptions. Therefore, the project went beyond obtaining teacher perceptions of the qualities of good citizenship, and began to look more closely at how they perceive citizenship is gained, enhanced and threatened.

Results are straightforward – both in terms of the questionnaire and interview data, and they reveal a clear picture of the notion of citizenship held by teachers, based on this sample. Prominent among the results is the firm belief that parents are the key influence in the development of citizenship, and that the availability, use and abuse of drugs is the biggest threat. Some significant questions are also raised. First, do teacher perceptions of qualities of, influences on, and threats to citizenship match what they do, or believe should be done, within the classroom? Perhaps, however, given the results of this research, the pivotal issue relates to how teacher perceptions and actions correspond to actual education for citizenship as addressed through the curriculum.

It becomes of paramount importance to determine if present efforts purportedly geared towards the development of good citizenship have as a primary focus the development of good, moral, co-operative *people*, rather than good *citizens*. Is the focus on the former without acknowledging critical dimensions which address, through the curriculum, the broader definition of the latter? This research suggests that the former is the current reality. That argument is based on teacher perceptions and the reality of citizenship as one of the cross-curricular themes. The latter were characterized by the National Curriculum Council as being one of the 'intangibles which comes from the spirit and ethos of each school' (NCC 1990, p. 10).

Contemplating this pivotal issue will determine the course of action. While reviewing the research results as presented in the next chapters, the reader is encouraged to consider these questions: are teacher perceptions of influences, threats and action related to the development of good people or of good citizens? What is the difference, what is the reality, and what should be the balance?

Certainly, clear provisions exist with regard to the formal condition of legal citizenship; however, the meaning, concept and practice of citizenship go far beyond boundaries related to where one is born or takes up legal residence. The meaning and perception of, and the actions related to citizenship appear to go far beyond a single, fundamental definition; yet the clarity of education for citizenship in terms of curriculum and teacher perceptions is decidedly vague. The research revealed in the following section confirms that indistinct nature of education for citizenship as it presently exists.

REVIEWING THE INITIAL RESEARCH

In the Citizenship Questionnaire (see Appendix), the intent of the first of the four sections under the sub-heading, Citizenship Questions, was to obtain a clear picture of qualities teachers believe constitute good citizenship. Based on the questionnaire and interview data provided by that initial inquiry, and with the confidence a combination of empirical and qualitative analysis allows, it can be stated that teachers in England have a clear tendency to view citizenship from the context of socially oriented perspectives.

Citizen-like qualities identified as most important by the teachers involved in this research project support the social dimension of citizenship first articulated by T. H. Marshall. The research lends credence to the current situation in which a majority of the public discussion related to citizenship occurs in the context of issues related to social welfare, volunteerism and community involvement. From both an empirical and a qualitative research stance, examination of the first segment of the project unequivocally revealed a profile consistent with the ideals of a nation built on the foundation of a solid social orientation.

EXAMINING PERCEPTIONS: THE NEXT STEP

So what is to be done with this knowledge? Does it alone provide enough support to allow tentative assumptions regarding what those same teachers think influences the development of 'good' qualities of citizenship or how these might be engendered in schools? While the initial analysis is enlightening with regard to teacher perceptions of good citizen-like qualities, it does not provide much practical information about what they believe should be monitored or put in place to support the development of good citizens.

Assessing teacher perceptions and identifying dominant social constructs was only the first step in a project designed to generate practical knowledge to inform how to proceed with citizenship education in this country. The next two sections on the questionnaire, in addition to the parallel interview questions, sought to delve more deeply in order to address a series of questions: Where did those perceptions come from? What contributed to the attitudes of individuals responsible for citizenship education in schools? Do perceptions match what teachers believe to be key influences on or threats to a child's citizenship? Do teachers play a role in the formation of attitudes towards citizenship in their students which is similar to how they themselves developed?

The second and third sections of Citizenship Questions were designed to investigate how perceptions were initially formed; then, based on their experience, to look at factors teachers believe impede the development of good citizenship. Developing another layer of understanding about where teachers believe their views originated may better inform how students' perspectives towards citizenship evolve – particularly since much of their education geared towards citizenship development, at least at school, is highly dependent upon those teachers.

Using Statistics to Assess 'Influences' and 'Threats'

In selecting the statistical procedures to use, we need to consider what it is we want to find out. In this case, through the use of a reliable survey tool, our aim was to learn as much as possible about what teachers believed to be critical factors in the continuing discussion about citizenship or, more specifically, what were teachers' views of the influences on and threats to the development of citizenship.

As with the first section about determining teacher perceptions of qualities associated with good citizenship, statistical analysis of the second and third sections first required the calculation of descriptive statistics. Descriptive statistics allow an immediate visual picture, followed by a deeper analysis of the organized data. Obtaining a broad representation of perceptions provides a firm foundation from which to view the overall research.

Teacher perceptions of the key influences on the development of their own citizenship, and teacher perceptions of threats to a child's citizenship were the general dependent variables in the second and third statement sections. As before, the six independent variables were obtained from the demographic information on the questionnaire. More detailed subgroup analysis (reported below in this chapter), further aimed to discover, for instance, if younger and older teachers, or perhaps newer and experienced teachers, tend to view influences and threats differently, and this provides a research base for discussing the implications of that information.

Given all this, from the informed perspective of both quantitative *and* qualitative analysis – what is it that the data tells us teachers believe are the key influences and major threats related to citizenship development? What exactly does the research say?

WHAT THE RESEARCH REVEALS ABOUT KEY INFLUENCES

Quantitative Results: the Empirical Data

Following their selection of choices in the segment asking for their perceptions of the qualities of a good citizen, teachers were asked to continue with the Citizenship Questionnaire by responding to the following statement: *'The following have influenced my citizenship.'* From a selection of six choices, on a scale ranging from strong agreement to strong disagreement, teachers expressed their personal perspective on the development of their own citizenship. Twelve areas of influence were provided in a menu of 'choices': parents, friends, brothers and/or sisters, religious leaders, television and/or films, grandparents and/or other relatives, guardians, teachers, head teachers or other school officials, extra-curricular activities, other students and youth leaders.

Descriptive statistics were calculated on the 12 item responses and then rank ordered by item means. The rank order of total sample for influences on good citizenship (see Table 4.1) provides a clear profile of the total sample's view of perceived influences on the development of citizenship.

Results were overwhelmingly clear. Parental influence emerged as the key influence by far, with a mean ranking of 5.47. This corresponds to the reported combined response in which 89 per cent of teachers expressed the overwhelming influence of their own parents in the development of their citizenship. The rank order by means further reveals that next in teachers' perception of perceived influences instrumental in the development of citizenship come friends (64.9 per cent), teachers (47.6 per cent), brothers and sisters (43.1 per cent) and extra-curricular activities (41.1 per cent).

The questionnaire offered a wide variety of categories of potential influential people, and while not all were school- or home-related, teachers' selections provide a clear direction in the way teachers think about influences. While parents certainly came out as being the leading influence in the empirical data, that does not mean adults in other roles exert no influence. What it means in *this* research study and based on *this* sample, is that those 'other' adults were not targeted by teachers as being key influences in the development of their own citizenship.

Table 4.1 Rank order by means of total sample of influences on good citizenship

| Variable | M | SD | Combined responses[a] | |
			f	%
Parents	5.47	0.83	601	89.0
Friends	4.81	1.05	436	64.9
Teachers	4.30	1.15	317	47.6
Extra-curricular	4.09	1.35	271	41.1
Brothers/sisters	4.09	1.45	266	43.1
Grandparents	3.82	1.51	239	36.1
Other students	3.68	1.28	181	27.8
Head teacher	3.21	1.35	112	16.9
Religious leaders	3.02	1.62	140	20.8
Television	2.97	1.33	82	12.3
Coaches	2.81	1.44	85	13.5
Guardians	2.60	1.58	63	13.9

a 'Combined responses' columns report combined frequency and percentage of respondents selecting choices 1 or 2. Of six possible choices, selection of '1' indicates 'strong agreement' with the item.

Qualitative approaches, such as interviews, allow researchers to discover additional information not addressed through the tool of a survey. Interestingly, interviews did not reveal anything particularly different from what was found empirically true about adult influences in the developing citizenship of a child. Further analysis, comparing and contrasting key influence responses with demographic categories, revealed nothing particularly significant in the way teachers view parental influence on their citizenship in terms of gender, age or experience.

Qualitative Results: the Interview Data on Influences

Based on the preceding discussion, it can be stated with reasonable accuracy that teachers participating in the questionnaire research are in wholehearted agreement that parental influence is a key component in education for citizenship. However, a questionnaire cannot shed light on how those influences may have come about, ascertain how early attitudes may have begun to form, or determine what parental conduct teachers perceived to have made a difference in the formation of personal qualities related to citizenship. Interview analysis can enhance the results of empirical research by providing some of the answers to those questions.

Individual interview sessions gave teachers the opportunity to discuss the development of their own citizenship and speak further about related issues in response to a series of open-ended questions. Specific questions were posed to 'start the conversation'. These included queries such as: 'When you hear the word citizenship, what comes to your mind?', 'In what ways are you a good citizen?', and 'Who helped you to develop or acquire those character-istics?' Comments meant to be representative of the interview research, and particularly representative of emerging perceptions, will appear through-out the ensuing discussion of key influences on and threats to developing attitudes towards citizenship.

Whether in the context of sharing personal experiences, or speaking directly about their work with students (responses were often intermingled due to the nature of the questioning process and the 'free flow' nature of interviews), responses correlate remarkably well with what was both sought and revealed by means of the empirical portion of the research. Inter-view results show that the groundwork of citizenship education is clearly laid at home, and one's attitude towards and actions related to citizenship reflect one's upbringing.

Before personalizing their comments, teachers tended to first speak in general about their view of what they considered were the qualities of good citizenship. In the context of discussing ways in which they believed they were good citizens, teachers often talked about how they felt they had developed or acquired those characteristics indicative of a good citizen. Teachers were mostly straightforward with their answers, identifying parents as a strong influence, as demonstrated by the following candid statement:

> I've got no doubt where it came from. It came from my father. I remember this from an early age when we lived in a Welsh mining village. My mother was less overtly political, but a decent human being: a kind person. The two of them have been the most influential without a doubt on my concept of citizenship and my concept of justice.

Such representative remarks were not uncommon in response to *'Who helped you develop or acquire those characteristics?'* – and are encapsulated in this further series of comments: 'To be honest, most of it was from my parents'; 'from my parents by example'; 'parents' influences in just terms of basic honesty and decency'; 'values of my parents and certainly the way I was brought up'. Results of the interview research further confirm the impact of parental influence already identified by 89 per cent of teachers completing the questionnaire in terms of the key influences on citizenship.

Clearly, and particularly in the context of how good citizen-like character-istics are acquired, it was succinctly stated by another teacher interviewed: 'Everything starts at home.' And while school as an influence received some passing mention, comments consistently harked back to earlier influences at home:

> In school we had certain rules . . . about showing respect. I am the person I am because of the rules that were instilled in me in school . . . and also because of my parents.

Upon analysing interview transcripts, two distinct strands emerged: the overwhelming influence of parents in their role of teaching what is moral and just; and emerging qualities of social consciousness as a parallel development. Both appear to be intertwined in teacher perceptions as correlated with good citizen-like qualities. The influence of parents is clear, and appears as a common thread in the text of teacher interviews.

> I feel they showed me a good example and they pointed me in a lot of appropriate directions spiritually, morally, politically.

When asked to reflect on where her sense of good citizenship came from, another teacher neatly summarized the general view towards parental influence.

> My own sense of right and wrong . . . I suppose that's something that I've had passed on from my parents . . . ultimately it does come from my parents.

Such perceptions are far from solitary examples. In numerous instances throughout interviews, parents were described by their offspring as powerful models of social responsibility. Evidence of the latter strand is demonstrated by the strong sense of social consciousness which teachers identified as significant in the youthful development of their concept of citizenship and, subsequently, their beliefs and actions as an adult.

> My parents used to have a shop, so you know we were serving people, so I was brought up in this idea, you know, serve; that very word, you know, to be of service to someone. Social responsibility was certainly part of my upbringing . . . strong sense of community atmosphere.

Rather than discussing citizenship qualities – in themselves or their parents, as related to such things as paying taxes, obeying laws, political involvement, or awareness of world situations – the majority of comments representative of parents as 'good citizens' were primarily related to how they demonstrated a sense of decency and community involvement. Highly typical of such views is this statement:

> My mother was a very upright, caring person, and she was very keen on doing things for people.

As demonstrated consistently throughout interviews, parents are perceived as models of decency, social responsibility and social justice. Based on the quantitative and qualitative results, such perceptions formed early have clear and lasting impact on the developing attitudes in their children of how a good citizen looks and how a good citizen acts.

It is interesting that the enduring nature of parental influence is noted by such a large number of teachers in the sample. Perhaps many reflected back on a youth they remembered as being characterized by a solid, traditional family. Most certainly, many individuals are brought up within a family atmosphere comprising a strong foundation and firm moral base. However, whatever teachers on the whole are remembering about influences on *their* citizenship, and whether or not their experiences are contradicted by those of the younger generation, the question becomes: are those perceptions as relevant for today amidst rising divorce rate and broken homes, dysfunctional families, and the increasing splintering of the once solid nuclear family?

This raises many very complex issues. Research has shown that family conflict is associated with mental health problems (Cherlin et al. 1998), crime (Lamb et al. 1998) and many other facets of life patterns (Gottman and Krokoff 1998; Nock 1998). However, while it seems obvious common sense to argue that parental marital quality and life satisfaction of children are related, there are very many other issues to consider (Gohm et al. 1998). Divorce is almost commonplace now; life within a family after divorce may lead to benefits for children; there are other important variables associated generally with the types of families who experience divorce, the particular circumstances of the breakdown and the impact upon the individuals within specific families. It can only be stated here that teachers see their own citizenship being intimately connected to the nature of their relationships with their parents. It is unsurprising, therefore, that one of the chief threats to citizenship identified by teachers is the problem of family conflict. Clearly, teachers recognize that the reality of many families today is not one that includes positive role models and strong influences towards developing a good citizen. Perhaps to bolster the power of that all-important home influence (or counteract those home influences characterized by 'family conflict', as demonstrated by expressed teacher concerns for today's student), the connection between home and school needs to be greatly augmented and addressed formally through the curriculum.

In response to questions related to those perceived elements in society which cause one to want to 'be a good citizen', as teachers spoke of their personal views interesting comments were made on the rewards and reinforcements of being a good citizen. Some clearly reflected the two strands noted previously – both the moral and the social awareness aspects.

> I suppose it's subconsciously you're doing things as your Mum would have wanted. I think the true citizen is one which doesn't look for

rewards or earthly rewards, but just does it to make themselves feel better.

> Rewards? I suppose it's because there's some morality involved that you believe it is right to be a good citizen so that as regards your conscience, you believe you're acting properly . . . So there's that moral payback.

Before proceeding to a detailed exploration of teachers' perceptions of threats to good citizenship, a few interview comments are particularly enlightening and are relevant to the discussion on how to best educate for citizenship. In response to being asked about the rewards and reinforcements related to being a good citizen, this teacher's response contains the essence of what it is critical to learn from the research:

> If people don't feel encouraged to be good citizens, the best you get quite often is you don't get caught.

Surely, it is our aim to go well beyond 'not getting caught' and, just as surely, that comment should be noted by curriculum designers.

Citizenship education does not develop in a vacuum; it is a concept that needs to be well defined, nurtured and encouraged.

> Some people would say that I'm a good citizen because I conform, whereas other people would say I'm a good citizen because I do more than I have to.

Is it a balance between that conformity (whatever that may mean in terms of a good citizen), and 'doing more than I have to' that we seek in education for citizenship? Examining that and a range of other issues and questions, as well as paying attention to the results of the questionnaire and subsequent interview research should be elements within the consideration of the continuing challenges related to educating for citizenship. There may be issues arising from these results which could lead to useful further research. For example, having become a good citizen, it may be important to explore the reinforcement of citizen-like activities. Paterson (1998) has noted that civic activism by teachers is felt to be beneficial to society generally but is also perceived by teachers as having a positive influence on the quality of their own teaching. He suggests that:

> The strongest correlates of high levels of activism were being male or female without children, having a strong sense of personal political efficacy, being more educationally experienced (for example, holding a promoted post or having taken a post-graduate degree) and (for the

more political types of activism) being more left wing and being more in favour of civil liberties.

(Patterson 1998, p. 279)

We need, perhaps to explore in greater depth the sorts of activities as well as types of people who help develop or reinforce good citizenship.

WHAT THE RESEARCH REVEALS ABOUT PERCEIVED THREATS

Combined Quantitative and Qualitative Results

The third section on the questionnaire was a statement intended to obtain a less personal, more professional perspective. Interview comments correlated well with what the statistical analysis revealed about teacher views in this context. In their discussion of influences on citizenship, teachers had frequently made reference to 'how things are today' for students.

In the third section, teachers were asked to assess what factors might, in their view, impede a child's developing citizenship: *'I believe the following are a threat to a child's citizenship.'* Teachers were to indicate their perception of possible impediments on the same 6-point scale, this time in response to 10 suggested threats: television and/or films, drugs and/or alcohol, peer pressure, sexual activity, negative role models, family conflict, school environment, excessive leisure time, unearned material rewards, and community environment.

Descriptive statistics were then calculated on the 10 item responses, then rank ordered by means. As with calculating perceived influences, the combined percentage of respondents scoring 'strongly agree' and 'agree' was also determined as an additional way of examining the relative perceived importance of items. These data are presented in Table 4.2. Rank order by means showing the combined percentage of responses provides a generic profile of the view of participating teachers by reporting their responses in descending order of their perceived importance.

Based on these empirical procedures, results are once again quite evident. Teachers perceive the major threat to a child's developing citizenship to be the contemporary, widespread, societal problem of drugs. This strong perception of the potential threat of drugs was followed very closely by the perceived danger of negative role models, and then family conflict, as potential obstacles in the development of good citizenship. While the former was the stronger perception, these two were very close in terms of actual numbers. Peer pressure followed as yet another perceived threat to young people in the development of citizen-like qualities.

Table 4.2 Rank order by means of total sample of threats to good citizenship

Variable	M	SD	Combined responses[a]	
			f	*%*
Drugs	5.11	1.13	516	76.8
Negative role models	5.08	1.06	513	77.1
Family conflict	5.06	1.03	517	77.1
Peer pressure	4.84	1.16	462	69.0
Unearned rewards	4.28	1.31	311	46.5
Community environment	4.06	1.37	279	42.0
Television	4.04	1.41	268	40.9
Sexual activity	3.76	1.37	199	30.2
School environment	3.56	1.50	199	30.0
Excessive leisure time	3.51	1.36	165	24.9

a 'Combined responses' columns report combined frequency and percentage of respondents selecting choices 1 or 2. Of six possible choices, selection of '1' indicates 'strong agreement' with the item.

The threat of drugs emerged from the analysis with a mean ranking of 5.11. This corresponded with the reported combined response in Table 4.2 in which 76.8 per cent of teachers expressed an overwhelming concern about the prevalence, and subsequent danger, of drugs in society today. It would appear that, based on the data analysis, there exists some contradiction in that some research suggests that certain sorts of drug use has been normalized and there is perhaps some encouragement in the media today towards the legalization of drugs (Measham et al. 1994; Robson 1996; Sell and Robson 1998). Certainly based on this sample, teacher perceptions do not reflect that contemporary discourse; but which has the most reality in how those issues are addressed in the curriculum? If there is much public debate related to legalization of and scepticism related to drugs, whatever teachers believe, should not the curriculum prepare students to face and engage in that debate – particularly if their teachers perceive drugs (and related issues such as peer pressure, negative role models, family conflict) to be a threat to education for citizenship? This clearly is a message for curriculum designers.

The rank ordering further revealed that in teachers' perceptions of threats, negative role models and family conflict (5.08 and 5.06 respectively) are extremely close, and share the identical and rather high cumulative response of 77.1 per cent. Further confirmed by the identification of peer pressure with a mean of 4.84, and cumulative response of 69 per cent, it appears that teachers perceive those people with whom we come in contact as critical influences in the development of citizenship, both in positive and negative terms.

While teachers identified drugs as the single most critical threat, in contrast the existence of excessive leisure time was deemed as least threatening with a mean ranking of 3.51, generating a mere 24.9 per cent cumulative response at the lower end of the rank order. Evidently, this factor was not thought to be a substantive threat to a child's developing citizenship.

If indeed the perception is that children today have excessive leisure time, whatever form that takes, it was not thought by teachers in this sample as a key issue in citizenship development. This is, however, interesting in the sense that drugs are perceived by teachers to be a key threat, and yet excessive leisure time is hardly mentioned as a related factor. It might well be worth further exploring the wealth of existing research related to drug use among youth and how it correlates to peer pressure, lack of direction, and young people having increased time on their hands compared to previous generations.

School environment and sexual activity appear at the very bottom of the listing of the threats to good citizenship. This supports the lower cumulative percentage of agreement as demonstrated in Table 4.2, indicating that teachers in the sample appear to believe these factors are significantly less threatening to the development of good, citizen-like qualities than those already mentioned.

The first section of the Citizenship Questionnaire asked teachers to indicate basic background information such as age, gender, and years of teaching experience. Statistical differences which emerged when comparing teacher responses to that demographic information in an analysis of subgroups are of some interest. Significant gender differences were found in relation to perceived threats of excessive leisure time, family conflict, negative role models, peer pressure, sexual activity, and television. In every case, men felt more strongly that these factors were threats than did women.

This finding is particularly interesting since these categories include some of the highest and lowest rated categories of threats to a child's citizenship as determined by this study. As already reported, negative role models, family conflict, and peer pressure – all selected more frequently by men – closely follow drugs as being the primary threat. In contrast, excessive leisure time, sexual activity, and television were among the lowest rated threats yet, once again, men selected these threats with greater frequency than did women.

While gender differences regarding threats to citizenship do exist statistically and appear well substantiated by the data, what they mean is not so easily determined. One might speculate that gender differences reflect the perspective from which male and female teachers approached statements designed to assess threats to a child's citizenship. Perhaps it could be said that men on the whole approached the questionnaire from the perspective of their personal experience. In other words, males may have identified the same impediments to the development of good citizenship that they encountered when they were 'coming of age'. This would explain the strength of their agreement, as well as the direct contrast with the female viewpoint. In comparison, women may have looked at potential threats from the viewpoint of an adult assessing existing threats to her students, rather than approaching the choice categories from a personal perspective.

Another interesting significant subgroup difference emerged with regard to the choice of drugs as a threat. This time, the difference was related to age, with younger teachers in the sample feeling considerably more strongly than their older colleagues about the danger of drugs, the highest rated threat to citizenship. The Background Information section on the Citizenship Questionnaire had requested teachers to indicate their age group in one of five categories. Of the five categories, it was the youngest teachers (aged 20–30 years) who felt much more strongly about the danger of drugs than did their counterparts in the other four groups.

Perhaps given the experience encountered by the past few generations with regard to this issue, the fact that younger teachers see the immediate threat of drugs is not surprising. It may be that theirs is a better knowledge and understanding of the issue, having observed the realities of the drug culture while coming of age themselves. From that standpoint, the educated young teaching professional may well be more cognizant of the prevalence of and the threat related to drugs in relation to the young people in their charge. While there may be other interpretations for the significant difference revealed by non-parametric tests conducted in the subgroup analysis, this perspective would certainly offer one way to explain the variance in terms of strength of opinion.

Whatever the meaning of any subgroup differences, whether based on gender or age, the empirical data distinctly shows that teachers on the whole are in strong agreement that drugs are a potential detriment in the context of educating for citizenship in a contemporary world. Furthermore, it demonstrates that negative role models, family conflict and peer pressure share almost equally in their view as potential threats. In a very real sense, these threats may be thought of as highly interrelated.

It could be easily surmised that negative role models and peer pressure are concerns well related to the key perceived threat of drugs, as both are potential components related to the issue of drug use (i.e. peer pressure to use drugs, negative role models involved in the perceived glamour of a drug-related lifestyle). As well, family conflict is often related to the abuse of drugs and alcohol. Clearly, teachers are concerned that these elements are a real danger to the development of the qualities of good citizenship. With an empirical basis in place in terms of perceived threats, interview results can support or challenge the quantitatively obtained information. In this case, interview data support empirical findings.

IMPLICATIONS FOR THE CURRICULUM

The challenge of good research is to not only examine an issue, but to present and articulate findings so that they are useful. Research is not, and should never be, an empty exercise. Rather, it should put results to work towards the purpose of informing direction. The findings in this research project should be taken into consideration in order to inform the direction of curriculum implementation strategies and frameworks to better meet the challenge of education for citizenship.

Research findings in this project tell much about what teachers consider are qualities of good citizenship. In earlier chapters, those perceived qualities were discussed in some detail. Constructs emerging from statistical procedures provided clarity in terms of where teachers stand – at least those teachers as represented by this sample. Based on the research, they stand squarely within a distinct concept of social citizenship; a concept accompanied by related views of social awareness, social responsibility, action, involvement and social justice.

The dimensions of research discussed in this chapter revealed additional information related to factors teachers consider consequential in the formation of good citizenship, as well as those factors considered most threatening to that development. This segment of the research project revealed that teachers consider the early influence of their parents as pivotal in the formation of their citizenship, and that the parental model most influential was that of a community-minded, socially involved, socially conscious parent. The research also tells us that teachers consider drugs as the biggest detriment in developing citizenship; and that related factors such as negative role models and peer pressure are real concerns.

Do we structure a curriculum entirely around perceptions of teachers, or, at the very least, consider those influences in the development of a curriculum formally designed to educate for a wider definition of citizenship? This research clearly reveals some sense of civic virtue, suggesting citizens as being individuals who advance beyond social awareness to the more tangible level of social 'doing'. Scholars earlier in this decade noted a distinct shift from a strict political literacy approach in the 1980s to a broader sociological definition which emphasizes the relationship of a citizen to society as a whole (NCC 1990; Turner 1993; Commission on Citizenship 1990).

CONCLUSION

'Education is clearly one way in which the foundations for citizenship may be laid and laid better' (Oliver and Heater 1994, p. 7). It is becoming increasingly evident that the meaning of 'education' in this context is broad; that education for citizenship commences long before a child formally enters the classroom. In this chapter, that fact is well substantiated. Issues were raised, questions posed and research discussed relating to how attitudes about citizenship are formed, what those attitudes are, what can get in the way of the formation, and what implications all this may have for the curriculum.

Based on this research, we have substantive information about the specific qualities teachers believe are critical to good citizenship. We are in possession of teacher perceptions which target parental influences as most crucial in the development of good citizenship, and drugs as the most dangerous threat. This leads to the obvious question: Is any of this information related to the curriculum in terms of education for citizenship? Is any of it taken into account in the classroom? And if it is not – then why not?

Within the foreword of the Speaker's Commission report presented at the beginning of this decade, Speaker Weatherill stated: 'Citizenship, like anything else, has to be learned. Young people do not become citizens by accident' (Commission on Citizenship 1990, p. v). Key issues emerge related to what it is exactly students are learning about citizenship. What standard, if any, is in place to ensure schools play an effective role in helping to produce good citizens; and should qualities, influences and threats – such as those perceived by teachers – be taken at all into account in the process?

Finally, and perhaps central in the examination of this issue, it is important to determine if present efforts towards developing good citizenship among our youth should focus primarily on developing good, moral people in a social context, rather than on addressing in a substantive manner those undertakings necessary to advance beyond formally preparing good *people* to the wider definition of developing good *citizens*. This is a question to which we should begin to turn our attention, for research results generated by this project very clearly support the former, and reveal the imminent challenge of the latter.

Since teachers, who work in daily contact with students, have identified specific factors as being important, influential or threatening to citizenship, it would seem to be prudent to take note of such information in the future design of the curriculum, and continuing professional education for their teachers as an enhancement of the present approach to citizenship education. The next chapter provides practical research-based information on putting the findings to work, and explores exactly what the research reveals teachers suggest be *done* in the classroom to contribute to the development of a child's citizenship.

5   What Sort of Work Do Teachers Believe Should Take Place in Schools to Promote Good Citizenship?

The intent of this chapter is to convey exactly what the primary and secondary teachers who undertook the survey and shared their thoughts in direct interviews are convinced must be in place, *from their perspective,* if schools are to have a fundamental impact on the development of what they believe to be good citizenship. It is important to bear in mind that the meaning of 'good' citizen is also a reflection of teacher thinking as reported by the research.

Analysis of the research in this project has revealed much about teachers and their perception of the qualities of good citizenship, what they believe to have been particularly influential in the development of their personal attitudes and opinions, and what they are convinced are key influences and threats in the development of a child's citizenship. Given all this, it is highly appropriate to view findings with the intent of exploring teacher suggestions and methodically moving towards implications affecting practice.

The very nature of the suggestions offered by the teachers asked to share pragmatic views reveals much about their understanding and orientation in the process of educating for citizenship. While this is not yet the place for speculative commentary, or discussion of direct implications for the curriculum, the results raise compelling issues in need of consideration.

The research clearly demonstrates a significant alignment on the part of teachers towards viewing citizenship roles and responsibilities from a highly social and relatively provincial perspective. The quantitative results also reveal an anomaly in that, while teachers targeted activities related to world-wide needs and responsibilities as a necessary and critical focus in the development of activities related to citizenship education, the preponderance of qualitative research results finds this aspect conspicuously absent. Instead, interview comments reveal an almost exclusively social and local view of citizenship education, with no substantive attention to that quantitatively identified focus.

Such knowledge can inform how to proceed in a variety of ways. Schools can follow the direction indicated by teachers – those individuals who are at this time primarily responsible for citizenship education – and institute activities teachers have noted would be the most helpful. Or, research can be considered by a wider audience to better gear the entire curriculum towards effective education for citizenship. What that looks like is yet to be determined, but close examination of the research results will most certainly aid in determining how teacher perceptions and suggestions fit in with the current intentions and realities.

RESEARCH GEARED TOWARDS PRACTICAL STRATEGIES

Quantitative Results: the Empirical Data

Following their selection of choices in the first three sections of the Citizenship Questionnaire, teachers completed the final segment of the survey – a section focused more on practicalities, but based on perceptions. The aim of this final section was to discover specifically what teachers believe should take place in the classroom that would be most helpful in meeting the goal of education for citizenship – at least their perception of what should comprise education for good citizenship.

The information sought was in direct response to the following: '*I believe that the following classroom activity(ies)* would be *helpful in developing a child's citizenship.*' Once again, teachers expressed their responses on a 6-point scale ranging from strong agreement to strong disagreement, and descriptive statistics were calculated on the eight item responses. A range of potential activities was provided in the menu of choices. These included activities in which the focus was on traditions and values, current events or history and government. Other choices involved activities in which a child would work on community projects, engage in problem-solving activities or use constitutional and legal processes. The final two suggested activities were aimed at a child's individual needs and interests, and those that focused on examining broader worldwide needs and responsibilities.

The resulting rank order of total sample for classroom activities (Table 5.1) provides an interesting profile of what teachers in the sample identify as the potentially most helpful activities.

The profile is largely consistent with what the research has revealed so far. Table 5.1 clearly demonstrates the emphases teachers believe most critical; however, just as clear are activities they appear to believe are unrelated or not significant in education for citizenship.

Based on the statistical analysis, teachers in this sample overwhelmingly targeted two specific activities as potentially most beneficial to developing good citizenship. Activities which look at worldwide needs and responsibilities, and those where a child would work on a community project were

Table 5.1 Rank order by means of total sample for classroom activities to develop good citizenship

			Combined responses[a]	
Variable	M	SD	f	%
Worldwide	5.02	0.94	498	74.0
Community project	4.98	0.98	481	72.0
Traditional value	4.88	1.03	460	68.3
Individual interests	4.73	1.12	408	61.0
Current events	4.60	1.00	374	55.9
Problem-solving	4.43	1.11	311	47.0
History/government	4.36	1.04	292	43.4
Legal process	3.84	1.12	180	26.9

a 'Combined responses' columns report combined frequency and percentage of respondents selecting choices 1 or 2. Of six possible choices, selection of '1' indicates 'strong agreement' with the item.

identified by teachers as the two most valuable activities. The former had a mean ranking of 5.02, and analysis of the latter revealed a ranking of 4.98. The higher mean rankings demonstrate that teachers tend to more highly value the worth of those activities related to worldwide responsibilities and community involvement. The rankings concur with the reported combined response for each at 74 per cent and 72 per cent respectively.

The two highest rated activities were closely followed by the selection of an activity in which a child would examine those traditions and values that shaped their community or country. This selection had a cumulative response of 68 per cent, demonstrating that teachers perceived it as being close in importance with the other two choices.

In contrast, activities with lower mean rankings, demonstrating that teachers view them as less significant to citizenship education, were those involving constitutional and legal processes. This produced an extremely low cumulative response of 26.9 per cent (and is remarkably consistent with the research results throughout this study regarding qualities of good citizenship, and as revealed through interviews). It is interesting that teachers in the sample appear to view activities involving knowledge and practice of such processes as *not* helpful in the development of citizenship. This is a strong indication that teachers perceive of citizenship as belonging almost exclusively to the social and moral domain. This is consistent with one teacher's statement: 'Teachers have always been reluctant to get into the controversial area of teaching politics.'

Upon comparing the demographic data from the Background Information section of the Citizenship Questionnaire with the empirical data of teacher responses, subgroup analysis revealed some interesting statistically significant differences. One puzzling difference emerged in the area of gender, as men viewed activities involving individual interests and activities involving problem solving as more important than did women. The reasoning for this is purely speculative and could be discussed and well supported, depending on the viewpoint one wishes to take. One might produce research to demonstrate a traditional view that men tend to be 'naturally' drawn to problem solving and working independently to approach problems; and yet that outlook could be as easily countered with comparable research highlighting the competencies of women in terms of problem-solving abilities. We have no desire to initiate a convoluted discussion of gender differences, abilities or controversy that is not pivotal to the aim of this particular research. It is perhaps enough to have noted the existence of a statistical difference in the subgroup analysis. It is left to the reader to determine the meaning of subgroup difference in this area.

Another statistically significant difference emerged in the area of activities involving legal and constitutional activities. Of the five possible age group categories in the demographic section, younger teachers who indicated their age as being between 20 and 30 years viewed legal and constitutional activities as being more important than did teachers from other age groups. It is possible that those who have more recently emerged from college or university were involved in the study of legal and constitutional activities, so would have naturally selected these activities as important. Or perhaps teacher training in the past decade has paid increased attention to legal and constitutional activities, particularly in light of the political activity during that past decade involving new emphasis on the European Community, economic challenges and the change in national political leadership.

A final subgroup difference emerged when analysing the category where teachers were to indicate the route they had followed in obtaining their training as teaching professionals. Significant differences were found among those who indicated their route to teaching as attending three years at university with a main subject speciality and then obtaining a PGCE. The significant difference between these teachers and their colleagues appeared in their preferred selection of the area of 'helpful' activities focused on history and government. Those obtaining their credentials through initial teacher training at a three-year, teacher-training college tended to select activities that aim at a child's individual needs and interests as being those most helpful to citizenship.

Perhaps these two statistically significant differences can be attributed to differing emphases between university and teacher-training college programmes aimed at teacher preparation. It is possible that there is a more explicitly vocational orientation to some programmes. Others may include heavier doses of history and government than do their counterparts, contributing to a better potential for orientation towards citizenship development. Possibly teachers attending less subject-specific teacher-training programmes tend to focus less on content area and more on the needs related to the learning process. None of these explanations is offered to indicate that one route to teaching is preferable to another. Rather, they are presented as a possible rationale for the noted statistical differences between the perceptions of these particular groups.

Qualitative Results: Examining the Interview Data

Attention now turns to what teachers in this sample determined should be in place in terms of specific classroom activities designed to enhance citizenship education. When conducting research using both quantitative and qualitative data collection, interviews have the advantage of being able to address some of the perplexities that can emerge from empirical analysis. In this case, interviews revealed some of their own perplexities.

Direct excerpts are provided from interview transcripts to clearly demonstrate the perceived importance by teachers of social doing as an important component in education for citizenship. Also provided is a 'listing' of specific teacher-generated suggestions which emerged, presenting substantive practitioner ideas which should be helpful in the design of future curriculum. At the very least, the kinds of activities that teachers suggest identify the existing gaps and impending challenges related to citizenship education.

Examination of the interview results will begin with comments related to the broader view of citizenship as encompassing social and political domains. It is interesting to note, however, that throughout the interviews, *far fewer* comments related to the political domain emerged than did those related to social orientation. The majority of teacher statements consistently reflected the more typical view that social behaviours as learned and practised at home and within a school setting are the most common focus in the 'teaching' of citizenship. These encompassed everything from collaboration, co-operation and listening skills to classroom management and behaviour policies.

The following statement articulates a broad view of citizenship as well as indicating the role of educators in preparing students to function as good citizens. This teacher's words suggest the importance of skills and knowledge in order to function as a good citizen in the social and political realm.

> My profession is that of schoolteacher and I believe I have an important role in trying to do something about the emerging citizen profile of tomorrow's adults: to maximize the learning outcomes of my students so that they can become stakeholders in our society as full participating citizens.

This statement serves as an introduction to the report of interview results for reasons other than its expressive nature. This is one of the relatively few remarks that extended the view of citizenship and the role of teacher beyond a purely 'social' view of citizenship, beyond a local view and, indeed, beyond the school building. However, even this articulate individual offered no substantive suggestions regarding what that 'something' might be, or how those 'learning outcomes' could be maximized or, indeed, what those learning outcomes are. Comments which expressed a philosophical rationale for addressing citizenship in school appeared infrequently throughout the interview transcripts, but in most cases omitted specifics of how these things might be delivered through the curriculum. Perhaps this is because though those teachers recognize the need, the structure for addressing it however is simply not there. The reality is that, as one teacher succinctly put it, 'Citizenship is the bottom item in your tray.'

Many interview comments focused on the need to raise awareness and do a better job of promoting citizenship.

> 'We just want to raise their *awareness*'; 'Civics and things like that . . . it's part of the hidden curriculum if you like and its something that needs to be more overt'; 'Be *aware* of political issues . . . so many kids haven't got a clue about the parliamentary system and what the political parties stand for'; 'I don't think it would grab their attention trying to explain the mechanics of voting or something like that . . . but certainly an *awareness*'; 'I would expect them to be *aware* of fundamental issues and concepts'; and 'Reinforce you have a duty, you know, in society.'

One teacher expressed a view that advanced a step beyond awareness and addressed how it is important for future citizens to understand that the world outside of their daily existence is relevant:

> that all that talking on the telly has actually got something to do with something [I've] studied; trying to get them to realize that to be aware of what's going on in the world beyond their village is really important.

Among the most perplexing statements was one that appeared to be a contradiction: a teacher stated the role of the school as critical in preparing citizens, but apparently saw no need for a framework to help accomplish it.

> I see what we do in school as providing the students with the tools of deciding how they would like to see their society when they are fully fledged citizens.

However, these words were immediately followed by this remark from the *same* teacher:

> But I can't see the point of having citizenship in the curriculum.

This raises issues not only related to how teachers perceive their role, but also asks the question of exactly what those tools *are* that they feel should be provided to students to equip them to make those wise decisions.

Many teachers made comments reflecting that, in their view, the idea of educating for citizenship is highly interconnected with expected behaviours, both in terms of compliance to rules and moral and 'right' behaviour. The school setting was the most common context noted for addressing those behaviours, rules and social interaction as part of educating for citizenship. Interestingly, one of the most commonly noted examples throughout the interviews was that a good citizen picks up litter: 'Seeing a crisp packet and putting it in the dustbin is a quality of a good citizen.' Many comments made directly in response to exactly how schools can educate for citizenship related to factors such as 'coming to class on time', 'following the behaviour policy', 'classroom management', 'school rules', 'taking pride in your school' and 'the absence of bullying and vandalism'.

Such behaviours and respectful adherence to policy in school, which was frequently noted as being a 'microcosm of society', were consistently identified as indicators of good citizenship-in-training. Teachers often noted the importance of the school community and ethos as paramount in the training of future citizens, commenting that 'students have to be active participants rather than passive'. Whether the illustration was that of involvement in the student council, participating in local elections at school or engaging in social interaction, the importance of school as a community was perceived by teachers as being the foundation of the process of citizenship education.

Moral and 'right' behaviours such as respect, co-operation and tolerance were also noted by a majority of teachers in the sample as factors critical to emphasize at school, and were considered part of the 'informal' curriculum of training good citizens: 'cooperation and collaboration would be part of the ethos of the school'. Working and playing co-operatively, learning to listen, and simply being courteous and considerate were characteristics frequently noted as being those essential to encourage at school as part of the process of citizenship education.

> A good citizen is someone who listens to other people, who doesn't try to impose their own values on everybody else, who is prepared to co-operate, who is someone with a bright outlook on life.

Interviews also revealed a perception that good citizens should be involved in the local community, and teachers often spoke of projects which involved students in social 'doing': 'we tend to address more of the community service bit than the rights'. One teacher noted that she would like to see the definition of citizenship more in line with responsibilities within the community. Many of that teacher's colleagues at other schools already involve their students in a variety of 'good citizen-like' activities outside of school, such as old-age pensioners' parties and working with local trusts and charities to meet community needs. It appears that teachers see citizenship as something which is given real expression in local terms.

Among the more substantive suggestions with regard to classroom activities teachers believe would promote good citizenship are those which advance students beyond the classroom and right into their local communities. However, one teacher's perception is that there should be more done in this area:

> I don't think we're achieved enough yet in terms of local community, both here as a school as well as home and society at large.

Whatever the extent of involvement in the local community, the evident perception is that this is the most appropriate direction for sound citizenship education. In fact, one teacher commented that she 'would like to see the definition of citizenship more in line with responsibilities within the community'. This social orientation is highly consistent with the analysis of teacher perceptions throughout this research.

Specific Classroom Activities Suggested by Teachers

Specific suggestions for activities in the classroom determined by teachers to be most helpful in developing good citizens reflect the meaning of what teachers perceive to be good citizenship. These suggestions tend to fall into specific categories. The first involves specific ways to 'develop an affinity with the community' through community service projects, many of which already exist as part of the culture of many schools.

Teachers suggest taking advantage of local contacts in the community to demonstrate links and create partnerships so that students develop a sense of the 'bigger world'. Specific ongoing projects were given as examples of what schools should be doing to promote citizenship in this area: 'a local cemetery project', 'donating to Oxfam' and 'charity appeals'. This kind of suggestion was encapsulated in the statement: 'Learning comes from doing.' This was echoed by another teacher who emphasized the importance of social action by stating that what we have to do is 'avoid having just a state of becoming rather than being involved in youth citizenship'.

Another category of suggestions involved the overall style and approaches that teachers should adopt, rather than mentioning specific activities. To enhance good citizenship, it was suggested that teachers act as good role models, personalize discussions and connect the curriculum to the 'real world', get involved in extra-curricular activities by doing things outside of the classroom with students, encourage students to be interested in politics ('a challenge really!') and, above all: 'Don't tell students it's citizenship: don't label it.'

Among suggestions that teachers determined would help promote good citizen-like qualities were classroom activities designed to develop a sense of interdependence, those that teach students to question, and those that look at a range of issues and teach students how to use debating skills. School administrators are encouraged to introduce departments to possible outside resources and bring people into the school to 'promote citizenship'. One comment revealed a school programme already well involved in this aspect:

> In school we arrange opportunities for students to have contact with a variety of people . . . to make the school culture more dominant than the peer culture.

Each of these things was noted as potentially helpful in addressing education for citizenship.

Citizenship education as presently approached in the National Curriculum is that of a cross-curricular theme without a clear structure. Interview results showed that while some teachers felt this was adequate: 'We don't need a programme, just use cross-curricular', others commented that PSE sessions 'might be used to some extent' to address citizenship-related issues. Still others felt that citizenship issues could be addressed in a variety of subject areas, but without suggestions of how that might be done. Others felt the need for more time and structure, the better to address citizenship.

> I would like to see in the National Curriculum more explicit guidelines so, for example, when one is teaching medieval realms in the Peasant's Revolt, opportunities are suggested for teachers to introduce human rights and community service.

EMERGING QUESTIONS AND ISSUES

Aristotle's view was that good citizens were most likely to emerge when engaged in the training and practice for a good and virtuous life (Heater 1990; Aristotle trans. 1967). The majority of teacher comments and suggestions deal with behaviours within a community, and clearly much of the focus is indeed on developing that 'good and virtuous' life. In many cases, suggestions are made in the context of the school community, sometimes branching out into the local community.

Referring to the quantitative analysis, the selection of activities reflecting the tradition and values of the community or country as being high on the list is provocative. One might speculate that, if the term 'community' stood alone, this activity might have rated even higher. The research would certainly seem to suggest that teachers may have selected it as a valuable activity primarily because it included the term 'community'. This is certainly not to imply that the tradition and values of the country are not held in high esteem, but rather that the tradition and values of the *community* as viewed in a more local context are regarded as an initial and primary consideration.

Further, in analysing questionnaire results, while selecting involvement in community activities seems to be entirely consistent with teachers' views (and subsequent suggestions) of what a good citizen 'does', it appears almost contradictory that the recommendation of world-wide or international projects was selected as a key activity towards developing good citizenship. This is particularly noticeable since only a single related comment regarding 'being good citizens of Europe' was noted throughout the entire transcript of interviews, and essentially no suggestions were made regarding activities addressing that wider view of citizenship.

Since this component does not appear anywhere else in the interviews and the discussion of activities to promote good citizenship, it might be surmised that simply including the choice of worldwide or international projects on the questionnaire served as a reminder to teachers who would otherwise not have thought of it. In completing the questionnaire, their response may well have been, 'Oh yes, that *is* important'; however, it may not be a factor that would have normally come to mind.

While quantitative analysis shows teachers rated world-wide needs and responsibilities as very important, the global factor does not appear to have a substantial place in the informal curriculum of education for citizenship. A broader world view did not figure in the activities suggested by teachers as being 'helpful' in the process. The traditional view of citizenship from a social perspective appears safely ensconced in a highly local context.

Reviewing the research results from this segment raises a number of questions and some concerns. Based on the data, teachers appear to conceive of knowledge directly related to the processes and administration of government, and learning to function as a political citizen, as not particularly relevant to citizenship education. Classroom activities selected by teachers in the quantitative portion of the research do not reflect as being particularly significant to good citizenship those citizen-like functions such as voting, knowing the process of law and of being well informed. Rather, the focus is on activities involving being helpful, courteous, moral, tolerant and socially conscious. These qualities are certainly not *un*-citizen-like qualities; in fact, it is highly desirable that a citizen internalize and be guided by such qualities. However, the definition of good citizenship should not encapsulate only these qualities, neither should they be exclusive.

It is possible there are a number of layers of citizenship at play – each considered important in some context, yet defined in very different ways. If this is the case, those layers might be grouped as moral, local, and national citizenships, with yet another layer reflecting a wider global context. Continuing the analogy, based on the research, the top layer would certainly be that of moral citizenship, closely followed by the concept of the local, and socially involved, kind of citizenship.

Acknowledgement of this latter citizenship would explain teachers' choice of world-wide projects as being a very helpful activity – possibly a result of the ongoing emphasis on the European Community, especially during recent years. No doubt teachers want their students to be aware of their membership in the wider community while still functioning primarily on the social, local community level.

If this paradigm is acceptable in the sense that a good citizen will have some involvement in all layers, the research demonstrates that the first two are well in place among teacher perceptions, yet the latter are *expected* to be viable parts of the curriculum. The challenge may be that while there will always exist some variance in perspectives, developing a balanced view and drawing from all four layers might be desirable.

> The majority of citizenship support materials for teachers . . . contain statement with little substance. The emphasis focuses on embracing a feeling for the variety of communities to which we all simultaneously belong: family, school, local, European, and worldwide.
>
> (NCC 1990, p. 3)

Without clarity in the curriculum, without a legitimate assessment structure, and particularly in light of the results of this research showing where teachers perceive emphasis to be necessary in education for citizenship (Baglin Jones and Jones, 1992), successfully addressing those 'layers' in a cohesive manner appears to be troublesome.

CONCLUSION

Empirical results suggest a dichotomy in that teachers advocate both community and international projects as being valuable, yet that wider scope has not appeared elsewhere in teacher perceptions which, according to this research, are firmly based in a local social orientation. Interview results tend to confirm the more provincial view, suggesting activities focused on the school community and the local community, but not substantially beyond. In addition, classroom activities suggested by teachers deal very much with small community co-operation within the framework of school as a 'microcosm of society'.

If certain elements have been identified through this research project by the very individuals charged with the delivery of citizenship education, then perhaps those elements should be considered in the design of the curriculum. However, it is critical to compare teacher perceptions and perspectives with what needs to be in place to adequately address citizenship education in this country. Revisiting aims expressed in *Education for All* serves as a reminder of the convincing rationale for the alliance of education and citizenship.

> Good education must give every youngster the knowledge, understanding and skills to function effectively as an individual, as a citizen in a wider national society, and in the world community.
>
> (DES 1985, p. 560)

Being given 'knowledge, understanding and skills' in order to 'function effectively' as a citizen in a variety of contexts presents a clear challenge to the educational establishment. This challenge is a huge one. Because 'many teachers tend to view the cross-curricular themes as foci running across the subjects at right angles, as warp the weft of the subjects, many more teachers appear to ignore . . . or be ignorant of them' (Ahier and Ross 1995, p. 2). This is of primary importance to those concerned about the sanctioned yet arbitrary manner in which citizenship is approached in schools.

Part III

What Is To Be Done? Ways Forward in the Development of Good Citizenship through Education

6 Action in Schools

INTRODUCTION

This chapter suggests various ways in which schools and others can further the possibilities of good citizenship and of education for good citizenship. Although there are many very difficult issues and serious obstacles to be confronted and overcome, successful teaching and learning in citizenship education can take place within our schools. It is suggested that there are positive opportunities for such work at a time when in many countries the language of citizenship is on the lips of high-status politicians and officials. In England, the context of this book, the commitment of the government in general and the publication of the Crick Report (QCA 1998) in particular, is to be noted. It is vitally important for everyone involved to seize this moment.

There are three main sections to the chapter. First, the means by which those responsible for the development of acceptable and valuable frameworks of citizenship education are explored. Second, we look at the structures that can be used within schools by heads and senior teachers and others to facilitate citizenship education. Third, there is discussion of the ways in which action can be taken by individual teachers working with pupils.

A number of preliminary remarks are necessary. Although the purpose of this chapter is to make concrete suggestions, this does not mean that a view is taken of teachers as technicians. This would be to negate the development of good citizenship education from the outset. Rather, there is an attempt to refer to a range of strategies which can be considered by teachers and others. These suggestions will be based at least *in part* on the research referred to in this book, without pretending that there is irrefutable objective data arising from our research which validates each proposal. They will also relate to work which has been undertaken elsewhere and has been reported as being successful. A final and vitally important point is the recognition that these suggestions in themselves cannot ensure that society is suddenly transformed into a vibrant democratic community. If it was so simple for action by teachers to lead to such dramatic results, then it would be appropriate to blame teachers when social ills appear. The authors of this book have no wish to add their voices to that blame which has been all too common in recent years. There is a recognition that it is extremely important for teachers to play their part, but there should also be at times an understanding that 'the concern is not with the desirability or expediency of education for citizenship but with the necessity of citizenship for education' (Griffith 1998, pp. 44–5).

WORKING PARTIES WHICH OPERATE BEYOND INDIVIDUAL SCHOOLS

There is an extremely disheartening recent history of educational reform in which teachers have not been treated as citizens. The research presented in this book does not explore policy processes but, nonetheless, teachers' views and experiences must inform policy development. Teachers reveal themselves in our data to be generally very positive and determined to make the world a better place:

> I'm extremely keen on this idea of being active in a society, being in it for certain reasons. I try to be a good neighbour. I try, and quite consciously, to be part of the local community because I wasn't born around here. And to a certain extent I want to put something back into the society now . . . I actually (amazingly enough) feel positive about paying tax because I feel I'm paying back in a way the number of years that I was supported. I've done a lot of volunteering . . . You've got to be able to say, Well, I could try and do it better, and the more you do that the more you realize how difficult it is to do it better [laughs] . . . As a citizen you can't just sit back and say they're doing it all wrong.

This positive commitment needs to be recognized. Moreover, to insist that teachers promote good citizenship while expecting them to accept disenfranchisement does not sit easily with the ambitions of citizenship education. Unfortunately, there is a plethora of evidence which supports the argument that disenfranchisement is in fact what has been happening. This sorry state of affairs probably reached its height under the term of office of the Secretary of State for Education John Patten when, for example, one reform which was to be piloted was declared – three months before the pilots even began – to be so popular that it was likely to be extended (Barber 1997, pp. 58–9)! Accounts of the making of policy and the misuse of evidence to promote specific curriculum initiatives are well known (e.g. Gipps 1993). Further, there is research data available supporting the rather depressing view that structural reforms relating to self-management have not worked to energize or empower those working in the educational service. Some of the most incisive criticisms of the ways in which education policy has been recently managed have been made by Stephen Ball, who sees the teacher being used in curriculum reform as 'deliverer, tester, technician'. He argues that in the new market-led education system, the range of teachers' roles was restricted to 'commodity producer, performer, entrepreneur'. And when teachers were managed, it was as if they were in a context where the key words were 'resource, accountable, cost' (Ball 1994, p. 49). It is clear that the reforms which aimed for 'increased participation in the governance of schools by lay people and the increased accountability of teachers' (Deem et al. 1995) have led in effect to marketization and a 'quangocracy' based on a powerfully negative critique of teachers.

How can this state of affairs be improved? One possibility will be to develop ways of working with teachers through initial and continuing professional development programmes. This is explored in detail in Chapter 7. Later in this chapter we will propose specific ways in which teachers can take action in schools. Something also needs to be said about the way in which the reform process is managed. We have already mentioned briefly in Chapter 1 the way in which the implementation of curriculum reform has changed from the research and development of the 1970s to the increasing centralizing force of the 1980s. Now, with the Crick Committee, we have returned to a working-party model, but one in which centralist force is used without very detailed guidance for teachers. Currently, there is a lack of discussion and controversy surrounding modifications to the curriculum. This could be seen as worrying for a number of reasons. It is possible that teachers simply cannot respond because of either exhaustion with the reform process or because of deskilling as a result of that process. Perhaps there is a refusal by teachers to engage explicitly in the public debate, as they simply get on with their work behind the classroom door. There may, of course, be a more positive interpretation which suggests that teachers are now more in favour of what is taking place. A professional policy-making process which involves consultation with – and perhaps direction from – an informed teaching profession is necessary in all areas and is essential in citizenship education.

Perhaps the most obvious initial way forward in the quest to create a more collaborative and generally professional policy-making process would be a public commitment. Key principles could include: respect for evidence; respect for professionals who should be consulted and whose work should be supported positively by advisory and evaluation – rather than inspection – teams; and an openness between the various parts of the educational community. Beyond such a statement of principles (which are so basic that to need to state them is a sign of the low status to which the profession has now been brought) there needs to be a strategy for effective action. The major part of this strategy would be to ensure an appropriate form of educational research: research which recognizes the complex web of technical and human factors; which sees as important who is engaged in the commissioning, writing and reading of the work; and which aims always to make an impact, even if only indirectly, on the real world of schools (Pendry and O'Neill 1997). This means not neglecting the vitally important fundamental research which explores the meaning of key terms and this book seeks to say something about that. But in this context it is important to have a research and development model which is based on consultation and leads to practical outcomes.

A number of ways forward are possible but it is necessary to disentangle certain tensions in the policy-making process. First, citizenship may be seen by curriculum planners as 'merely' a goal. It is a good thing which emerges once a pupil has been educated. This leads to many warm words about the value of citizens and citizenship in a democracy, but does not recognize what should be done by teachers and pupils. Ultimately, if the emphasis is placed on goals only, 'citizen' becomes synonymous with 'human being' and, once the rhetoric has cleared, there is little that can be done. There is a need for more attention to be placed on the process of becoming a citizen. Some good work is taking place in various subject areas which is leading to a better grasp of what it means to understand key ideas (e.g. Lee et al. 1996). It would be useful if there were similar efforts to develop understanding of what citizenship education means.

Another key tension for policy makers in this area to overcome is ensuring that high status is achieved for citizenship education but also that a meaningful model is developed. Currently, there is a plethora of working groups operating in overlapping territories. The experts on moral education may, unless the terms are defined carefully, stray so far into citizenship education that there is no clear difference left. Support from the Secretary of State for Education and Employment is vital and welcome. The guidance from David Blunkett to Bernard Crick that the advisory committee on citizenship should concentrate not just on political literacy but also on social and moral behaviour and community involvement led, unsurprisingly, to that three-pronged framework being endorsed by the committee. The framework does have merit but, for example, it omits anything very explicit to do with identity. The rationalization for the chosen model may need more argument than currently exists. The achievement of high status is necessary but not sufficient.

It is vital that the ideas for citizenship education are coherent and that teachers see those principles and concepts as being capable of being transformed into action. Normally, those who drive curriculum reform are not teachers. Teachers are busy enough teaching young people without also taking responsibility for all the thinking and writing that needs to be done to clarify and promote citizenship education. However, even with teacher representation on curriculum reform groups, it is possible to see a gap emerging between the tidy, near-rational thought of the advisers and the messy practical world of classrooms (Davies 1993a; 1993b). The long list of aims and objectives set within an overall target of extremely grand purposes which characterize educational reform documents sits rather uneasily with how lessons are actually planned and taught. Unless teachers are allowed the space and time to operate within the broad statements and to create practical ways forward, little or nothing will actually happen.

Finally, recognition needs to be made of the length of time needed for reforms to work. Professional educators, however, often find themselves faced by reforms which are initiated by party politicians, who are always aware of the ticking clock. Hesitate and the moment will be lost: another crisis will shift priorities; another election will remove them completely. While the broad framework can be agreed in a fairly short space of time, a number of years will be needed for real work to take place. The framework for citizenship education needs to be agreed, and teachers and researchers allowed to explore it and make it work over a period of time. Something similar to the review of the National Curriculum as undertaken by the Dearing Committee which led to a five-year period of no change would seem to provide a common-sense way forward.

SCHOOL STRUCTURES AND PROCEDURES TO PROMOTE CITIZENSHIP EDUCATION

A school as a whole can work to ensure that citizenship education is more than an idealistic unrealized ambition. The status of the work needs to be emphasized. One of the most obvious ways to do this is appointing a senior member of staff with a clear responsibility for citizenship education. That does not mean giving one of the deputies yet another job to add to the many he or she already does but, rather, announcing a high-profile initiative which involves regular, frequent and meaningful consultation, target setting and review. The co-ordinator should have a responsibility to liaise with national and local groups in the furtherance of education for citizenship. Effective communication, which has in the past been conspicuous only by its absence in relation to the promotion of political education and the low-status cross-curricular themes, should be a key priority (Davies 1993a; Whitty et al. 1994). An early priority would be the identification of elements within a particular school having citizenship education potential. The following areas readily suggest themselves.

The Hidden Curriculum

The term 'hidden curriculum' was first used by Jackson (1968) and, according to Meighan (1986), can be defined as 'all the other things that are learnt during schooling in addition to the official curriculum' (p. 66). As such, it can be given expression in a large number of ways acting, for example, through how space is used within the school by certain groups, time-tabling (which lesson normally appears in the prime slot of first period on Monday morning and which in the doldrums of last period on Friday afternoon), and the ways in which people speak with each other. If pupils stand when a teacher enters the room, address adults as 'Sir' or 'Miss' and defer to prefects, who are a small elite appointed by teachers to help general discipline, then significant lessons will be learned about the nature of the relationships within the school. There are a large number of writers who emphasize the importance of the ethos of the school (see a review of literature by Mellor and Elliott 1996) but remarkably little evidence to suggest the precise nature of its impact (a rather isolated example of some research is John and Osborne 1992). The teachers in our sample certainly recognized the role of the hidden curriculum. Most of our teachers spoke more about the general exercise of influence rather than the use of precise curriculum strategies. A typical view was that:

> The school is the great shaper because clearly the influences that operate on children are with them throughout life.

Unless this potentially vital area of school life is managed and explored then opportunities for citizenship education will be lost. The following areas are commonly used by heads and others to influence the hidden curriculum.

Defining Democracy, Involving Staff and Others

Trafford (1997), an innovative head who has reformed the school of which he is a part, has suggested that democracy means:

> a considerable degree of consultation, a right for individuals to speak their minds, whether or not they agree with the official or majority line of the school, and . . . an implication that the rights of the individual will be enshrined while at the same time being balanced with the needs of the community as a whole . . . [and] . . . the expectation of active participation by all those involved.
>
> (Trafford 1997, p. 8)

The above definition is (within the normally expansive rhetoric employed in debates on citizenship education) very limited, but it may be of great value. This definition does not require the school to rework its management structure completely. If such worthy but fundamentally limited and realizable objectives are used, there are fewer opportunities for disillusionment. It certainly complements the general position of our teachers who wanted to work with others:

> I think I identified with people who were struggling to make their mark or even change their lives in some way . . . '60s and '70s idealism, you see [laughs]. I thought you could make a difference – still got it.

However, we do not argue that teachers are consistently demanding a more democratic form of school governance. There were very few comments about that. This raises, potentially, a significant area for further work. If there had been evidence of demands for greater democracy, the necessary scale of change for schools should not be underestimated. The discussion by Trafford shows that there are very real threats to entrenched positions if this definition is taken seriously. Perhaps teachers recognize the difficulty of making significant shifts from existing positions. Nevertheless, it is possible for schools to consider greater involvement of staff. Perhaps this is what Crick meant by his statement that a change in political culture is required. Even when having pupils' as opposed to staff's involvement in school governance, there may be great challenges in developing a more democratic community. The very demanding outline of a discipline system based on a commitment to ensure justice through an approach emerging from the Universal Declaration of Human Rights is likely to be valuable (Cunningham 1992). The determination to pursue fairness through managing difficult incidents within a framework of investigation, resolution, restitution and sanctions is ambitious but emerges from the day-to-day working of a school. As one of our teachers said:

> I don't feel we should say to kids these are the rules and you should accept them. They need to see that every rule has a purpose . . . Once you stop giving these reasons to kids then I think you're asking for trouble.

Another commented:

> I want them to be able to be responsible for what they do, to accept the consequences of what they do and to be aware of other people. And I think if they can do those three things then I think I'm promoting citizenship.

For many of the teachers, education was seen in a particular way:

> Education is a crusade to me. It's a social crusade with young people. It's not about subjects. Subjects are important but in the end I want to produce youngsters by the age of 16 who are honest and reliable and then can go out into the world.

One way of encouraging a greater sense of responsibility might be to allow students to choose more of the courses they follow – an initiative which may lead to harder and more effective work. In general terms, Harber (1995) has suggested that there are a number of very important benefits of such work for the whole school which include: better rule keeping; improved communications; increased sense of belonging; better decision making. More specifically, it seems improved examination results are achieved, at least for some, when this approach to running a school with the intention of respecting and developing citizens is taken (Trafford 1997).

Involving parents and others in the local community in a way which is more significant than simply asking them to fund raise is an important enterprise which has links with some of the community education initiatives of the past (e.g. Ree 1973) and which fits neatly with the communitarian agenda of the present (e.g. Etzioni 1995). Developing a proper system for involving teachers and pupils in the community is of vital significance. Many of our teachers spoke about the importance of narrowing the gap between school and the local community. The evidence presented in Chapter 5 shows just how important teachers regard the potential of community-based education. One of the three strands for education for citizenship emphasized by the Crick Committee is involvement in the community. It is noticeable that an increasing number of publications reflect on the issues associated with community involvement (e.g. Reeher and Cammarano 1997; Rimmerman 1997) and, despite the potential disadvantages, it can be very valuable. The obvious disadvantages which teachers have to avoid in creating 'service learning' is to ensure that the ideals of young people – their wishes to help and to make a contribution to the community – are not exploited at a time when there are increasing numbers of old people needing attention and a perception that the welfare state is becoming too expensive to afford. Stradling (1987) makes a very strong case for political education on the grounds that issues can be tackled most effectively when people can readily see the need for some sort of action. As well as the voluntary projects assisted by organizations such as Community Service Volunteers, it is possible to point to other forms of successful action projects, for example, one involving liaison between a primary school and a local council which leads to the improvement of a park and its play facilities (QCA 1998, p. 26).

One of the most significant ways for local people to become involved in the life of the school is through the work of governing bodies. Their powers have recently been more sharply defined and expanded. There may, however, be dangers in expecting too much from governing bodies. It is perhaps significant that there were very few comments from teachers about the role of governors in citizenship education. Involving a few people on the governing body may not necessarily lead to a closer integration between school and community. Perhaps governors are not truly representative. A takeover of the school by the local professional elite is not to be welcomed. Further, there is a suspicion that at least some of the Conservative reforms were driven by a desire to control schools rather than develop democracy. The teachers would be more closely watched, responsibility for school buildings in need of repair would be transferred, while key curriculum decisions would be made centrally. There is a real fear that many governors were not active citizens in ways that were altogether valuable. Deem et al. (1995) have questioned: 'whether school governors are indeed acting as empowered citizens in the community or whether they are merely state volunteers' (p. 157).

However, if parents and others can act as representatives of the community then this not only presents chances for the school to be improved but also allows them to enact a process of citizenship which is both useful for them and for others to follow. A good deal more work on the role of governors and the way in which they interact with others is needed before we can be sure that they can contribute usefully to citizenship education, but there does seem to be some potential for positive work to take place.

Whole School Events

Schools regularly make use of special local and national events, including the commemoration of anniversaries. It is important for teachers and others involved to relate their selection of an activity to a particular aspect of citizenship and to ensure that the way in which the activity is undertaken is appropriate. It can appear odd (to strengthen the arguments made above about the hidden curriculum) if, for example, assemblies are used merely to harangue pupils about the benefits of democracy or, more common, if classroom work becomes something which is simply unrelated to the real world. While these special days and events can have tremendous value there is evidence of less desirable practices such as contributions of pupils' money being made – without their having been consulted – to organizations such as, for example, Amnesty International. This seems to run counter to the promotion of a genuine democratic understanding. Further, if there is an intention to promote intercultural understanding, little will be achieved by putting on displays which are nothing more than exhibitions of costumes and artefacts.

That said, there is value in celebrating special days, and those schools who formally remember, for example, United Nations Day or the life of Martin

Luther King are making important statements about the value of democracy, tolerance and the development of a pluralist society, as well as giving pupils key academic information and an insight into related issues. The development of awareness of key documents such as the Universal Declaration of Human Rights can be achieved through special events. Beyond specific anniversaries, other useful activities can be developed. One school from whom some of our interviewees for this project were drawn organized a very successful 'Democracy Day' (Davies et al. 1998) which provided pupils with opportunities to learn in an active and stimulating way about discrimination, aspects of justice and the legal system, embryo research and the workings of a House of Commons debate, along with arguments over the nature of punishment in schools. In addition, the pupils took part in a mock election. The events were regarded positively by staff and pupils; useful links were forged with people within the local community; and, as the day was evaluated by staff from the local university, there were opportunities for the school to reflect on how to develop future work. Even if answers could not be immediately forthcoming, interesting questions arose such as: Why was the Day better regarded by girls rather than boys and better received by older rather than younger pupils?; and, Was the working-party approach to the organization of the events the most appropriate and likely to bring most long-lasting benefits?

One of the main ways in which schools choose to celebrate democracy and to provide some opportunity to teach their pupils about the democratic system is to hold mock elections. This is one way to counteract the relatively low emphasis (according to the data presented in Chapter 5) that teachers placed on constitutional and legal processes. Old-fashioned civic education in the form of lessons about the British Constitution have long since been rejected in favour of a more active, realistic and worthwhile approach. The use of mock elections is now so common (including in our research schools) that there are major national and international institutions who work explicitly in this field and are able to provide advice and practical resources (e.g. Federal Trust 1998). These are some points to be considered when holding such elections:

- *Rationale and objectives* Have a clear rationale for the event and include learning objectives both for political learning and also for learning in other more formal parts of the curriculum. Consider what activities will be included, the time allocations needed and the methods of evaluating the event.
- *Issues* Explore with pupils the kinds and range of issues over which the election is to be fought and decide whether real or imaginary parties are to be represented.
- *Election process* Brainstorm what is to be involved in the election process and have an action plan and clear timetable for events on polling day.

- *Candidates* Devise with pupils a straightforward system by which candidates will be chosen, for example, they could produce a manifesto, then be nominated formally by three classmates and supported by two others from other years in the school. Decide how candidates' campaign teams will be chosen/allocated and the types of activities they will follow.
- *Information and publicity* Consider the possibilities of advertising posters and of developing a newsletter to report on the campaign. Campaign teams might also write publicity leaflets, hold meetings, address the school assembly, make tape-recorded mock broadcasts and videos to simulate use of commercial media. (All of these activities provide valuable links with English, technology and media education.)
- *Results* Decide how the results will be presented and discussed. Identify a range of factors that teachers and pupils can use to evaluate the success of the election and the work of all those involved. For example, they could consider the criteria used for a poster that had attracted maximum attention; discuss factors which had influenced the production of the liveliest and most effective speeches; and identify and demonstrate the skills needed for effective involvement in a debate.

School Councils

One of the key features of Trafford's (1997) attempts to democratize his school is the development of a school council. His and the school's commitment to the council can be seen despite (or, perhaps because of) the criticisms of it. Perhaps one of the functions of the democratic system and of politics itself is to find appropriate ways of reconciling conflict. The council finding itself attracting criticism may be a sign that it is being used actively in the resolution of real issues. Of course, if the council becomes merely a way of letting off steam, if it is unrepresentative, and seen to deal only with 'acceptable' and trivial issues, then it will not have made things better and may have made the situation worse. Teachers in our sample referred positively to school councils but were keen to make it clear that they present particularly difficult issues for schools. Some referred rather vaguely to the need to give pupils 'guidelines to work in'. Some explained the tension between wanting to promote citizenship education through a school council and recognizing the complexities of action:

> Pupils are encouraged to make decisions and they're encouraged to meet as a group to argue the case, to report back to the people they're representing about issues relating to their life in school. Having said that, there is a huge constraint in school and there are few no-go areas laid down by the head . . . I think we tend to address . . . responsibilities rather than rights. Because, of course, the rights are threatening to the

staff and to the school if you pursue that too far. But it's more subtle than that. It's not so much a knee-jerk reaction to, you know, the kids aren't going to run the school, but it's actually quite complicated. The ramifications, if you like, of decisions that are made become quite complex and its easier often to say, 'No, you can't talk about that' than actually to get engaged in a big dialogue and explain why. That can actually be more frustrating than just saying, 'That's a no-go area'.

But school councils, at their best, can develop communication skills, improve peer relationships, stimulate creativity and improve pupil behaviour and commitment to school (Haigh 1994; Gorman 1994; Siraj-Blatchford 1995). Deciding how many representatives from each class might be on the council, the qualities representatives might need, how they might be selected and the frequency of meetings provides an interesting and useful context for citizenship education. The issues which are discussed (such as girls' football or the lack of it, dinner-time behaviour, uniform, assemblies) do matter to children and give an opportunity for some discussion. There will probably be a need to make clear the parameters within which the council can operate but this can be an advantage in the same way as is learning how important are the rules of parliamentary procedure. Anybody in 'real' life cannot say just anything and, if handled professionally, pupils will learn better about how to operate in political situations.

Providing International Opportunities

There is some uncertainty within the data about international work. The results in Chapter 5 show that quantitative data gathered by means of the questionnaire recognized the importance of 'world-wide needs and responsibilities' while the qualitative interview data showed variations between teachers. These factors may be related, at least in part, to the long-standing debate about the meaning of citizenship between those who prefer to stress the importance of membership of a polity with attendant rights and responsibilities, and those who wish to emphasize the more affective approach which suggests the importance of making links with other countries or areas and pursuing ideas associated with, for example, the nature of identity (Wringe 1998). This is a crucial distinction and will affect all that teachers and others think and do about citizenship education. The strength of membership of a polity is that it contains the implications of what can concretely be done. There clearly is a set of legally enshrined rights and responsibilities and citizens can develop knowledge and skills to ensure that justice takes place or, at least, legal procedure is followed. However, the advantage of keeping one's feet on the ground can at times be outweighed by the absence of a dream of making the world a better place. There is, of course, no need for these hopes and ideals to be targeted or realized in international settings only.

It is perfectly possible for vitally important work to take place without ever leaving the confines of one's own area. Indeed, it seems the primary teachers' relatively greater emphasis on affective approaches in local contexts was evident in the research.

It is, however, easy to demonstrate that work in the international area is becoming increasingly easy to manage, and that it can be very rewarding for teachers and pupils. It is no longer difficult for very positive links to be forged with teachers and pupils in other countries. Osler and Starkey (1996) have written about the work that can be done when teachers are brought together; and now that the European Union is so actively promoting European citizenship there are numerous case studies which are available for others to consult (Davies and Sobisch 1997). Using e-mail and the Internet means that geographical travel is not essential (Austin 1995) and the exchanges need not be restricted to Europe (e.g. Bennell et al. 1996).

Action by Individual Teachers

Of course, the activities described above can only be of any benefit if individual teachers are fully engaged. It is teachers operating within structures that will make things happen. The hidden curriculum, the school council involve individuals. However, teaching is a profession where autonomy is still extremely significant and, to use a cliché, once the classroom door shuts the individual can operate in a variety of ways. This has always been true but may now be particularly so as teachers retreat away from the inspectors to do what they feel is most needed.

A fundamental approach to actions which could be taken by individuals would include that of regarding the teacher as generator of new ideas and activist for change. Citizenship education has, at least until recently, often been seen as being of low status, conceptually confused and confusing, and of high risk for those teachers who explore controversial issues but gain no reward because of the absence of a proper career structure in this area. If a teacher wanted to take action in the classroom there were obstacles to be overcome, among them, for example, a prohibition by a deputy responsible for curriculum arguing there was simply not enough time. In such circumstances, there are specific political skills a teacher could employ. For example:

- The head, senior management team and governors should be targeted, and persuaded of the importance of citizenship education.
- Teachers, parents and others should be made aware of the central definitions of citizenship in a way which makes it clear how good work can be achieved.
- The presentation of action plans is shown to be already comfortably within the school's aims.

- The current high-status nature of the work should be stressed, with reference to the work of the Crick Committee.
- Attention should be drawn to research which recognizes the professionalism of teachers when dealing with sensitive and controversial material (e.g. Stradling 1984).
- Above all, it is necessary to have stamina in persuasiveness and a tactical awareness of when it is important to make concessions.

When action is being undertaken in classrooms, much that is familiar within the normal work of teachers applies to citizenship education. One of the most common ways of proceeding is to engage pupils in discussions of controversial issues. There is good guidance about how to proceed. For Rowe and Newton (1994) the key points are:

- To encourage involved discussion from the maximum number of pupils.
- To use open-ended exploratory questions.
- To press children for reasons.
- To discuss whether some actions are better than others.

Guidance on the teaching of controversial issues has been included in the report of the Crick Committee (QCA 1998), with suggestions for general teaching approaches relating to the 'neutral chair' of the Humanities Curriculum Project; the 'balanced' approach, which could be expressed as the devil's advocate technique; and the 'stated commitment', which is used as a tactic to promote discussion. Obviously, most teachers use a mixture of these approaches, depending upon pupils' needs and their stage of learning and the nature of the issue. It would, for example, be fairly ridiculous to continue to use the stated commitment approach when all pupils have in the first few minutes expressed their agreement with the view being proposed.

The Crick Committee has proposed a four-part framework which identifies: key concepts; values and dispositions; skills and aptitudes; and knowledge and understanding. Teachers will need to examine these lists carefully to assess where in the curriculum and how best they should be taught. Some of the items can be taught in one subject area better than in another. A school may decide, for example, that Britain's parliamentary, political and legal systems could be referred to in history lessons, whereas the placing of 'judging and acting by a moral code' seems relevant to a wide range of areas of school life. For a teacher in the classroom (as opposed to any wider role they take within the school) there will be a need to make clear to pupils what is being taught and in some if not all cases, the assessment system in use will reflect the priorities. This is important to emphasize as history teachers – who many assume will be in the forefront of the citizenship education initiative – have at times revealed themselves to be in practice more committed to teaching about the past than using the past for the purposes of exploring citizenship (Davies 1997). That said, the data presented in Chapter 5 shows that many of our teachers did give examples of how history lessons could help promote citizenship education:

> I was very keen to do the French Revolution as the topic and you can bring in political ideas there and the notion of liberty.

> We teach the Chartists and, you know, we look at what people were demanding and we also look at did they have a right to demand it, and then the kids go and do their own charter. What would they demand? And then we actually have a discussion about that and we'd say what sort of things are really sensible things.

The above provided an interesting contrast with some other lessons in which teachers were prepared to talk about the relevance of the processes of learning more than the content or concepts of material studied. Co-operative work in mathematics and the general advantages of being well educated, for example, were briefly discussed by some teachers, as opposed to an in-depth consideration of the sorts of mathematical knowledge which may be directly relevant to citizenship education (Frankenstein and Powell 1994).

There is already a large amount of resources for classroom use. In light of the increased emphasis upon citizenship education there will surely be many more produced in the future. For primary schools, lists of available resources can be found in Edwards (1993) and Rowe and Newton (1994). UNICEF has produced material focusing on children's rights (UNICEF 1990); Addis (1992) has produced a collection of stories; Joyce's (1994) resource book explores values education. For secondary schools, the Law in Education project materials are useful; there are packs by the Children's Society (no date) and Lloyd et al. (1993); the Exploring Citizenship pack (no date) examines public services; and the Towards Citizenship pack produced by the Council for Education in World Citizenship (1997) consists of nine modules including ones on the community, the environment and international understanding. Oxfam (1997) has published 'a curriculum for global citizenship'. The Federal Trust (1998) has produced a series of booklets and packs on various aspects of citizenship around the four key themes of learning to participate, investigating the institutions, discussing policy options and learning from the lessons of the past.

Many teachers said that good citizens were not motivated by the search for rewards. However, it seems, if only on the basis of common-sense reasoning that it would be possible to use assessment methods sensitively as a means of recognizing achievement. At the moment there are remarkably few positive developments, and very radical thinking may be required if citizenship education is to be taken seriously (Whitty et al. 1996). Few of our teachers were able to suggest ways forward. However, it is possible to see much good work in citizenship education being perpetrated through the study of traditional subjects. But 'themes' and 'subjects' do have very different conceptual parameters and one needs to be particularly alert to the nature of intended learning outcomes and appropriate assessment methods in order that valuable work should occur. In subject lessons such as English or mathematics, the knowledge relevant to citizenship education will need to be stressed and the way in which it will be assessed should be made clear to pupils. There may also be a need to make time available for pupils to consider what they have learned in a number of subjects in relation to the learning outcomes. It may be appropriate to record achievement by using systems of profiling. Beyond learning in the classroom there should be opportunities for activity in the local community and elsewhere, which will require careful supervision so that sufficient flexibility is allowed together with a rigorous appreciation of the relevance of that work to the learning outcomes. Finally, it will be a major task to ensure that this form of assessment is recognized by universities, employers and others. Although it is possible that employers may be more interested in school leavers' attributes as citizens rather than in their knowledge of academic disciplines, there will be much work needed to discourage the drawing of inferences from traditional qualifications and looking towards what young people actually know. In other words, currently we allow selectors to make imaginative leaps about a person's capabilities on the basis of their achievements in fields not directly related to what it is a candidate may be being selected for.

CONCLUSION

Citizenship education is now enjoying a much higher profile than it has done for some years. There is the possibility of professional action. The obstacles are challenging but more can be done by curriculum groups, schools and teachers who wish to contribute to the strengthening of a democratic society.

7 Action in Programmes of Initial Teacher Education and Continuing Professional Development

If valuable, professionally based and explicit citizenship education is to have any chance of becoming a reality there is an obvious need for teacher education to be reformed. This need should be recognized in England where there has been a low-level, or, perhaps, even negative relationship between teacher education and citizenship education in recent years. There is already recognition of the need for such reform in a number of countries, including those which belong to the European Union and Council of Europe (e.g. Fogelman 1995) and in Australia (Nichol 1995). There is no reason why England should continue to insist on different practice from other countries. Its teacher education programmes should allow for the promotion of good citizenship.

This chapter begins with a brief summary of some recent events and trends which suggest that it has become difficult (at least, perhaps, until very recently) for teachers to become involved in preparing themselves for citizenship education. Arguments and recommendations are then developed to show what could be done to improve this situation. The professional development needs of all the partners are considered (teacher educators, teachers and student teachers), with particular attention being paid to three overarching areas (contacts and resources; access; and process), and three issues which are perhaps more specific (knowledge, teaching and assessing).

THE RECENT HISTORY OF TEACHER EDUCATION RELEVANT TO CITIZENSHIP EDUCATION IN ENGLAND

While there is, of course, much to praise in the work that has been done in recent years by teachers and others, it seems uncontroversial to assert that there have been many obstacles placed in the way of those who seek to develop good professional practice. Some mention of the unprofessional way in which education has been managed in recent years has been made in Chapter 6 and much more could be said about this unsatisfactory state of affairs (Lawn 1996). The area is complex and it is very important to emphasize that it is not the intention to make mere party political points within any criticism of recent policy. There has been an understandable determination to improve standards. Whatever political party had formed the governments of the 1980s and most of the 1990s, it is likely that radical reform would have been attempted. James Callaghan's 1976 speech at Ruskin College, Oxford, is suggestive of the sort of approach that would have been used had Labour achieved office. The consequence of the radical action that did take place was a collapse in morale and a perceived attack upon the autonomy of teachers. This is obviously related to debates surrounding citizenship.

The reasons for the very unhelpful stance taken by the Conservative governments are not entirely clear. Teacher education was regarded by the Tories as highly significant and was, in the form of Circular 3/84 (DES 1984) the first area of education to be reformed in the contemporary context. Perhaps the need to influence the economy (Gleeson 1987), the desire to bridge the perceived moral gulf in society through the new ideology of the 'new right' (Healey 1990) and the simple urge to exercise power in whatever area of public life had so far been unreformed (Lawton 1992; Davies 1993c) meant that action would be taken. The sort of action that did occur included one Secretary of State arguing that teacher education was in the grip of those who held to the orthodoxies of the past (Clarke 1992). This was taken up by right-wing polemicists who were eager to argue that students who followed initial teacher education courses would only be encouraged 'to waste a year undergoing a period of Marxist indoctrination' (*The Spectator* 1993, p. 5).

Elliott (1993) has usefully sketched three formulations which characterize a range of perspectives in teacher education. First, he outlines the Platonic or rationalist view of teacher education, which is now the outdated version of what many initial teacher education courses had to offer: 'good practice consists of consciously applying theory' (Elliott 1993, p. 16). Once an initial phase of teacher education has been undertaken and a theoretical background established, individuals can then be left to direct their own professional learning within, consequently, a voluntaristic pattern of in-service provision. The second model seems to be what we have experienced in recent years and is described by Elliott as the social-market view of teacher education as a production/consumption system. Learning outcomes are perceived as being essentially behavioural and competences are established which in essence are discrete practical skills. (Although a recent semantic shift has taken place, insofar as official documentation now refers to standards as opposed to competences, little of substance seems to have altered.) There is the strong implication here that 'the significance of theoretical knowledge in training is a purely technical or instrumental one' (Elliott 1993, p. 17). The school is to be put in charge of this development of behaviourist skills, employing higher education staff as they see fit. Even the title of the co-ordinating government body (the Teacher *Training* Agency), which keeps teacher education apart from higher education, is unhelpful and deprofessionalizing. The consequences of this sort of approach (i.e. Elliott's second model) to preparing teachers for citizenship education are alarming. The gradual decline of interest in something so fundamental in teacher education as equality of opportunity illustrates the need for reform. Circular 3/84, which has been referred to above in negative terms, still included a useful reminder that:

> Students should be prepared through their subject method work and educational studies to teach the full range of pupils whom they are likely to encounter in an ordinary school, with their diversity of ability, behaviour, social background and ethnic and cultural origins. They will need to learn how to respond flexibly to such diversity and to guard against preconceptions based on the race or sex of pupils.
>
> (DES 1984, Annex criteria for the approval of courses, para. 11)

In 1985, the Swann Report (DES 1985) included very positive encouragement that consideration should be given to pluralist issues within the central and compulsory core of all initial teacher training courses. The DES circular of 1989 (DES 1989), which tightened regulations in what some felt was an unhelpful way, nevertheless still included a section which insisted that:

> courses should prepare students for teaching the full range of pupils and for the diversity of ability, behaviour, social background and ethnic and cultural origins they are likely to encounter in ordinary schools . . . Students should learn how to guard against preconceptions based on the race, gender, religion or other attributes of pupils and understand the need to promote equal opportunities.
>
> (DES 1989, p. 10)

However, by 1993 it was being suggested that the wording of the guidance and the context in which it appeared meant that there was in fact an omission of *any* reference to equal opportunities (Siraj-Blatchford 1993, p. 91). The most recent documentation (DfEE 1998) may show some recent improvement by insisting that student teachers should set 'high expectations for all pupils, notwithstanding individual differences, including gender, and cultural and linguistic backgrounds' (p. 14) and that they are 'committed to ensuring that every pupil is given the opportunity to meet their potential and meet the high expectations set for them' (p. 16).

However, Elliott's third model (which he describes as the 'Hermeneutic View of Teacher Education as a Practical Science') seems some way off in initial teacher education, although he sees it as being used for in-service work. He argues that there 'has been the adoption of classroom and school-focused action research approaches which highlight the role of "teachers as researchers" in effecting improvements in practical situations construed as complex, ambiguous and unpredictable' (Elliott 1993, p. 17). There may be some value in developing new qualifications for subject leaders and head teachers. It is useful that efforts are being made to link initial teacher education with continuing professional development so that a more coherent and rigorous programme can be promoted.

However, currently there is a crisis in teacher education. The recent history of this area is characterized by: a negative interventionist strategy by central government, based on a lack of trust in teachers and teacher educators; the development of behaviourist competences which require compliance rather than professional thought and action; and immense practical difficulties relating to a serious teacher shortage. The latter is perhaps the most worrying of all issues and may emerge directly from the failure to treat teachers as citizens. If this is the case, it should be regarded as a matter of urgent priority that the notion of teacher as citizen is promoted. The Development Education Association (DEA 1998) has suggested that teachers should become active global citizens working towards a more sustainable and equitable future. They have the support of key government advisors (Michael Barber spoke positively at a DEA conference about the importance of such visions) and, given the nature of our research evidence reported earlier in this book, it seems likely that teachers would find this commitment to citizenship attractive. Specifically, the DEA has proposed that students of all new subjects will be able to:

- articulate their contribution to the spiritual, moral, social and cultural development of pupils
- participate actively in developing their own contribution to education for active global citizenship
- develop their practice of active learning to encompass models of democratic participation which foster pupils' autonomy and responsibility
- demonstrate their own role in helping pupils to increase understanding of the social, political, economic and environmental contexts in which they live.

(DEA 1998, p. 3)

This way of focusing on teachers' concerns is likely to do more to attract people into the profession and to improve the quality of life in schools, as well as raising standards in particular academic subjects, than any amount of behaviourist brow-beating. There should be official guidance for teachers and student teachers which concentrates on this aspect of teachers' roles and there should be explicit recognition of and support for teachers as citizens. This, of course, does raise potential difficulties. There is the possibility that some may come to regard such a role as being an acceptance of responsibility for all society's problems and, by implication, a preparation for receiving the blame when, inevitably, those problems refuse to go away. It needs to be stated clearly that teachers' potential (and willing) contributions to such matters need to be developed in some detail. There needs to be an explicit recognition in teacher education programmes of citizenship education, and (while avoiding the worst excesses of the competences route which has been mentioned above) we need to know what sorts of knowledge and skills are required and what sort of evidence is needed to demonstrate an appropriate level of teachers' and students' achievement. The way in which that work is to be perceived would be part of a restitution of teachers' standing in the communities they serve. It would move us away from the unrealistic limiting of the role of being 'merely' a subject teacher (no teacher can ever work so simply and narrowly) or as being the current scapegoat for almost all difficulties in the light of failure in all sides of relevant debates to understand the sorts of contributions that can be made.

DEVELOPING CONTACTS, CREATING AND ACCESSING RESOURCES

The three groups of teacher educators, teachers and student teachers all need to be considered but we begin with comments about the former – not to suggest that they are somehow more important but, rather, to insist that learning within higher education does (in line with the recommendations of the Dearing Report) require some explicit attention. Teacher educators themselves need professional development. A very clear account is available of an extremely valuable initiative involving 22 university departments of education in 13 European countries (Osler and Starkey 1996). The programme described meant that:

> Although few participants had experience of working in a transnational project, within three years a Europe-wide network of staff and student exchanges had been set up and a new teaching module was devised and available to each of the participating universities.
>
> (Osler and Starkey 1996, p. 103)

Activities for the participants included discussions to explore the meanings of the four key areas of the project (learning democracy, social justice, global responsibility and respect for human rights) and the identifying of professional opportunities and obstacles which would need to be addressed if useful work could be developed. The work was undertaken collaboratively and there was a feeling of professional and personal support within the groups. The specific outcomes included the establishment of the joint module referred to above, which included desired learning outcomes (e.g. 'Students should be able to express informed opinions in defining and discussing issues of . . . citizenship and social justice'); key themes (e.g. 'Understanding the importance of individual participation in a pluricultural democracy'); and pedagogy (e.g. 'To be consistent with the desired learning outcomes') (Osler and Starkey 1996, p. 112).

A similar but larger project involving 84 institutions in 24 states is co-ordinated by Ross (1998). This project is titled 'Children's Identity and Citizenship in Europe' and began work at the end of 1998 and is intended to continue for at least three years. It aims to:

- survey curriculum provision for studies in socialisation and social learning in higher education institutions in Europe
- describe and analyse different practices across Europe in the development of citizenship in children and young people
- record and analyse children's and young people's accounts of identity and nationality in a European context.

(Ross 1998)

As result of the work it is hoped to:

> develop European-wide shared teaching materials for modules and courses in higher education that draw on the similarities and differences between practices in states and regions. These will contribute to the development of new courses and more informed professional training for those involved in pre-schools, schools, social work and youth work.
>
> (Ross 1998)

Opportunities for teachers are similarly available through involvement in European initiatives. The Council of Europe and the European Commission offer numerous programmes, some of which are obviously and explicitly focused on teacher education, while others allow for the development of projects which almost inevitably promote teacher education (Davies and Sobisch 1997). The three current action programmes are Leonardo da Vinci (vocational education and training); Socrates (general education) and Youth for Europe III (non-formal youth education and activities). Although the former can relate to citizenship education, it is probably more likely that the latter two programmes will provide most opportunities. Socrates allows for the establishment of transnational projects, the mobility of teachers, students (although not school pupils) and other educational staff, and for exchanges of information. This is done through three chapters. Chapter 1 is known as Erasmus and encourages transnational co-operation between universities and the mobility of students. Chapter 2, Comenius, relates to school education with a focus on multilateral school partnerships, the education of children of migrant workers and other initiatives associated with intercultural education, and the updating of and improvement in the skills of educational staff. The third chapter deals with horizontal measures which focus on languages, open and distance learning, adult education exchanges of information, study visits for decision makers and recognition of academic qualifications.

Youth for Europe III has five actions which seek to promote and assist:

* intra-community activities directly involving young people
* youth workers
* co-operation between member states' structures
* exchanges with non-member countries
* information for young people and youth research.

It is also possible to develop co-operative work with partners outside Europe, and there are, for example, projects funded at least partly by the European Commission involving Canadian educators working with Europeans in mobility programmes. It can be very worthwhile to look to as broad a range of organizations as possible. UNESCO is very active in ways which relate to teacher education for citizenship (e.g. Harber 1997). The International Bureau of Education (based in Geneva) has since the mid-1990s produced valuable information and advice about citizenship education. There are many non-governmental organizations which also provide resources. The School of Education at the University of Ulster has produced material for teachers relating to, separately, values and controversial issues (Montgomery and Smith 1997; Logue no date). There is a huge amount of useful material in related fields such as values education and intercultural education. Developments in other countries can be valuable for teachers wishing to develop something themselves, with perhaps the series of four packs on civil, social and political education from the Department of Education and the National Council for Curriculum and Assessment in Eire, and many booklets and other guides from Northern Ireland on education for mutual understanding being worthy of particular note. Organizations such as the Citizenship Foundation, the Council for Education in World Citizenship, the Association for Teachers of Social Sciences and the Politics Association have good publications, manage valuable conferences for school students, student teachers and more experienced staff and can be very helpful in informal ways when approached by individuals. The *Social Science Teacher* (ATSS), *Talking Politics* (Politics Association) and perhaps to a lesser extent *Pastoral Care in Education* (the journal of the association of the same name) are tremendously useful for keeping teachers up to date. The Centre for Global Education based at the University College of Ripon and York St John produces a human rights education newsletter that gives invaluable information about current publications and events for teachers.

Increasingly, the internet is both an excellent source for specific materials that can be turned to good advantage and is also an effective means of achieving the global contacts with individuals, movements and causes which citizenship demands (Ball 1997; Canfield 1997; Rimmerman 1997). Simple searches when using the internet can reveal large amounts of material for teachers, ranging from academic papers on the meaning of citizenship education to very specific lesson plans. Some careful narrowing of the field of interest may be necessary – a search completed during the writing of this chapter revealed over 17,000 sites. This is reassuring to those who suggest that there are resources available but it also suggests that some sifting is needed. Perhaps a useful starting point would be to look at something like the civnet resources which are produced by the American Federation of Teachers' Educational Foundation. Its directory of civic education organizations and programmes can be found at http://civnet.org/orgprog/orgsprogs/op-icc.htm.

Access to Teacher Education

One of the most obvious obstacles to the development of citizenship education in schools is the limited extent to which teachers are allowed to become appropriately educated. At its most basic, this means that we must ensure that appropriate people are allowed and encouraged to join the profession. A new kind of teacher is needed: one with an academic background that puts him or her in a particularly good position to approach citizenship education confidently and skilfully. Currently, there are few courses available to graduates from philosophy, political science, economics and sociology. The Graduate Teacher Training Registry's (GTTR) guide for applicants who wished to enter courses in 1999 showed only six institutions offering places in social science, and one offering places in sociology. The details given in the guide make it clear that students entering such courses would be also expected to teach another (National Curriculum) subject, and/or to teach in non-compulsory contexts. In other words, currently the rhetoric is strong for the promotion of citizenship education while at the same time those most likely to be able to make a good contribution are, in practice, excluded from becoming teachers. There is some informal anecdotal evidence to suggest that some institutions who may receive applications from, for example, politics graduates wishing to train as history teachers, will not wish to accept them as the boundaries of the National Curriculum subjects are drawn unhelpfully narrowly.

As well as facilitating the admission to training institutions of those types of graduates who could make citizenship education a reality there is also a need to ensure that the standards and other guidelines are altered for all teachers so that the importance of citizenship education is made clear. This has been partly discussed above in relation to the significance of equal opportunities. It may also be possible to include in guidance for initial teacher education some instances of contemporary contexts and skills related to experiential learning and the teaching of controversial issues.

For those who are already teachers there is an urgent need to consider their appropriate access to further professional development. The recent introduction of qualifications for subject leaders and head teachers could offer a useful way forward. It is also to be welcomed that with such measures as student teacher profiling it may be possible to build progressive links between initial and continuing professional development. However, there is some evidence that teachers are not so much educated as prepared for inspection. There is an increasing focus on 'proper' (i.e. not cross-curricular activity such as citizenship education) subject-specific guidance with less attention being paid to whole-school matters. The standard five days in-service training provision is increasingly being taken over by individual departments. With the disappearance of advisory teachers, the delegation of inset budgets to schools as opposed to local education authorities, and the re-invention of advisors as inspectors, teachers are thrown more on their own resources than hitherto. Beyond these worrying contextual concerns is the debate over what sort of education needs to be provided. Should it relate to awareness raising, increasing motivation, developing knowledge and skills, or all three at once? What needs to be done so that some means of agreement between policy makers and teachers can develop? Who needs to be involved in such a process: is the school rather than a university or LEA the best focal point of such work? (Kinder et al. 1991) Simple answers cannot be developed to such complex questions which go to the heart of educational change. But it is essential to consider first just the obvious issues of who is available to teach citizenship education and who is receiving appropriate professional development. At the moment, the answer is rather depressing for those who aim to achieve fundamental change.

The Process of Teacher Education

If we are to take seriously the notion of teachers as citizens then it must follow that the process of teacher education must be appropriate. Some comments have already been made in this chapter about its importance. The projects which involved European colleagues working to promote better citizenship education were not organized so that experts could lecture novices, followed by testing of accurate memorizing and practising of the behaviours specified. The recognition of the need for this sort of work is becoming more obvious (Harber 1994; Molestane 1998). There is some recent evidence from school contexts (Trafford 1997) that a form of democratic in-service education can work and lead to 'mainstream' academic standards being raised. There needs to be an explicit consideration in in-service work of how the school can come together to think about its ethos. The ways in which policy decisions are made and the nature of classroom management that is actually and rhetorically promoted are some obvious examples of what needs to be discussed. Simply, schools need to find a way to focus on the always difficult issue of practising what they preach.

A number of democratic teacher education programmes which have been researched are showing impressive results for both the teachers and their pupils (e.g. Ryan 1996; Rainer and Guyton 1999).

There will, however, always be dilemmas in resolving the tensions in a programme that aspires to be in some way related to democratic processes and outcomes between curriculum design, 'classroom' authority and management of the seminar/workshop room. It is inadequate to pretend that the process of citizenship education is not problematic and potentially extremely controversial. Harber and Meighan (1986) have outlined a continuum on which there are five points illustrating the general typology of educational ideology in teacher training (p. 180). Putting aside the use of the word 'training', the typology is as follows:

1 A tutor-directed programme: an expert informs novices.
2 A consultative programme: a timetable is prepared by the tutor and will only be altered if that person agrees.
3 A general timetable is followed but there are opportunities for students to follow their own activities. Some consultation between tutor and student takes place to ensure some coherence.
4 Each individual designs his or her own course while the tutor adopts the role of guide and senior learner.
5 A collective democratic learning model is chosen. The group draws up its own agenda and decides priorities. The tutors are senior learners but they do not necessarily have the right answers and they use their own voices among the many.

Harber and Meighan argue that the first and fourth models are not congruent with political education. They also raise a range of other important issues about, for example, the extent to which group decisions can always be democratic. In today's climate, such radical action would be accepted only if modified in certain ways. Nevertheless, some way forward must be found if we are to escape the negative mechanistic managerialism that characterizes at least some of the current practice in teacher education. Perhaps the very nature of the activities and targets that are developed could help to square the circle. Some comments are made below about the sort of knowledge and understanding, skills and assessment frameworks which could be developed. Primarily, there should be an ethos of collaboration in which the shared task of promoting appropriate understanding and skills in citizenship education is always the first priority.

Promoting Teacher Knowledge for Citizenship Education

The data in this book shows that teachers are not familiar with the key aspects of citizenship education as characterized by theorists. This in itself may not matter if there was also a lack of confusion, wide knowledge (even if of a particular type) and skilled teaching. However, conceptual confusion and lack of widespread action is in evidence. If reform were to be attempted without paying due regard to what teachers currently know and understand, little would be achieved. Any action that is taken needs to be developed co-operatively if our comments about process are to be respected. In the light of the research presented in this book, we may now be in a marginally better position to promote certain sorts of knowledge and understanding. We do not argue that all the recommendations which follow are based squarely on the data, but we would like to suggest that they may be factors which others would want to consider.

The first obvious but significant point to make is that teachers and student teachers cannot be treated exactly alike. Our data, particularly in Chapter 4, shows that there are different priorities and conceptions, depending upon various factors. Teacher education programmes need to take account of these differences. Perhaps some general input is necessary, for example, by means of a cross-curricular initiative, but it is possible for some subject groups to be able to take a lead at certain times within a school or within a programme of initial teacher education. It may be worthwhile not to develop stereotypical assumptions. For example, the history student teachers are not always fully ready to take such a lead role – perhaps linguists may be better able to draw from their experiences of communicating positively with and learning about others (Campbell and Davies 1995).

A certain amount of personal knowledge is necessary. We do not suggest that this needs to be done by focusing on 'the inner self' (Kragh 1995; Voiels 1996). Rather, it may be useful when, for example, developing citizenship education through geography, to use students' own experiences of such formative events as migration in their own lives and in the lives of family members (Gonzalo and Villanueva 1995). Similarly, Rey (1991) and Davies and Rey (1998) have explored with student teachers of history some issues relating to family histories in an attempt to strengthen their understanding of and potential for citizenship education within an intercultural framework. This examination of what it means to be involved in citizenship education is, when used cautiously and professionally and with the permission of the participants, entirely appropriate for teacher education but may be far too intrusive or complex for school students.

It is necessary to ensure that the sort of understanding that is explicitly targeted in teacher education programmes relates to what the data in this book has shown to be in need of urgent attention. All three areas of Crick's three-pronged framework (social and moral responsibility, community involvement and political literacy) have associated knowledge and under-standing which can be targeted, and these areas are discussed in this chapter. But it is the latter of the three which is most likely to be neglected. This situation may change if the suggestions made in this chapter for enabling graduates of disciplines such as politics and philosophy to enter initial teacher education to become citizenship education specialists are imple-mented. But it will still be necessary to ensure that all teachers have at least had an opportunity to explore key concepts such as democracy, citizen-ship and pluralism. Without the minimum of a basic introduction to the fundamentals of citizenship there is little hope for altering the current situ-ation, in which teachers who have never explored the meaning of citizenship are drafted in to teach it due to the availability of a few 'free' lessons of their specialist teaching time (Davies 1994a).

Specific connections between 'mainstream' subjects and citizenship educa-tion should be explicitly made during teacher education programmes. There are many examples of various specialist subjects being linked with citizenship education. Mention has already been made above of history and geography. It is also not difficult to find teacher education courses which explore modern languages (Brown and Brown 1996) or environmental education (Lyle 1996), or maths, science and music (Conley 1991) – areas which are not normally thought by some to be relevant to citizenship education. If work in these fields was developed and an awareness of the key elements of citizenship education (whether it is formulated by Crick or elsewhere) was generally known and accepted, it would be possible to undertake rather more meaning-ful curriculum audits than is done currently.

Further, teacher education programmes should make it clear that some knowledge of the communities in which citizenship education is taking place is essential. Of course, there are (as has been made clear earlier in this book) a number of different communities within any area. The impor-tance our respondents gave to the links between family and citizenship, and the necessity of teaching citizenship through community involvement, means that some training must be given on knowing the community. Teachers and parents need to recognize their joint responsibilities and find ways of working together. It is not being suggested that teachers are to become some sort of social worker, but the notion of teacher as citizen is important and some elements of training from related fields may be useful. Attachment during training to a community group could provide useful opportunities. There could be great value in encouraging teachers and student teachers to learn about the educational aspects of certain organiza-tions in the community, asking them to consider the best way to promote links between local groups and schools and the best way to liaise with indi-vidual family members of school students and then requiring a self evaluation of their citizenship skills in a setting other than a school. Expanding a teacher's role in this way would not be very controversial, given the links that are regularly established in school–industry schemes. References made earlier in this chapter to Youth for Europe III show that resources are available for this sort of work in a European context.

Teaching Citizenship

There is a range of activities which student teachers commonly undertake in existing programmes which need only slight alteration to make them directly relevant to teaching citizenship. At the start of a course, for example, it is standard practice for observation of experienced teachers to be undertaken by students with their being told to look at or for particular aspects of educational work. It would be relatively straightforward for students' attention to be focused explicitly on citizenship education, perhaps exploring, for example, classroom climate or reviewing published materials to evaluate their potential effectiveness. Issues shown by research directly targeted on citizenship education to be particularly difficult even for experienced teachers could be highlighted and discussed. Some of these issues include the extent to which teachers tend to alter the substantive content of the lesson in light of their knowledge of pupils; the way in which similes, metaphors and analogies are used; and the way in which the trade-off is resolved between content coverage and pupil involvement (Dunkin et al. 1998).

Whether students or experienced staff are teaching, existing professional standards could be drawn from to identify particular areas which need to be practised. This is not to suggest that there is some sort of level which must be reached, and strict observance of one 'right' mode undertaken. Rather, there could be opportunities for different groups of school students to be taught a range of citizenship-related topics in various ways. There would be encouragement for variety and innovation within a climate that, following discussion, had been deemed appropriate for this sort of work. There are good reasons to suppose that this sort of variety could be achieved by teaching overseas as well as in the immediate area. Involvement in wider European contexts is likely to become easier and the rich potential this has for citizenship education should be exploited. The community projects which have been briefly alluded to previously could be established. Perhaps most importantly, there could be an element of research, or at least semi-structured investigation, into an aspect of a teacher's work in the classroom which had been self selected following supportive discussion with an advisor.

Assessment and Citizenship Education

Two key issues are raised here: the importance of developing teachers' roles in creating and sustaining links with the community; and assessment of citizenship education knowledge, teaching and assessment practices. Of course, no more than a brief outline, rather than a complete resolution, of some of the problem areas can be given here.

Much has been made in this chapter and elsewhere in this book of the necessity of a broader role for teachers in which they are seen again as key members of the community. This may seem initially to raise very many difficulties for assessment. If, simplistically, we aim for a teacher as citizen, does failure in a teacher education course mean that one is somehow a noncitizen? Of course, it does not. Assessment is a context within which those who are concerned to promote citizenship education can work positively. It should not be controversial for a student teacher and more experienced colleagues to show that they are able to fulfil this broader community role. If they fail to do so, this would not affect in any way their legal rights and obligations, their identity or self worth. The role of teacher as citizen is already accepted implicitly by the teachers in our sample. They did not often see their citizenship as deriving from their paid work, but this seemed often to be more due to a sense of modesty or uncertainty about the nature of being a citizen. To be sure, not all were involved in community projects and still fewer in programmes or campaigns related to political literacy. But they were supportive of the aims that are regularly mentioned in citizenship education programmes, and it would be possible for abilities to be recognized should schools or teacher education courses actually seek to bring them into being. This would, of course, not mean that teachers were expected to follow a particular political line. Rather, they would have the opportunity to become involved in, for example, a community project in the ways outlined above and reflect upon the citizenship education potential of such work. A profiling system which encouraged an explicit focus on students' actions related to community life could provide a way forward. Perhaps, at least initially, this could be kept within the fairly narrow boundaries of the school or university community, or even more narrowly within the sort of examples that students brought into their teaching. However, we should not always want to be so cautious. Assessment of active intervention is obviously something which is already at the heart of teacher education programmes. We cannot pretend that we are unused to assessing practical performance. Community involvement is a fundamentally important part of citizenship education and is already practised widely (Rimmerman 1997; Reeher and Cammarano 1997). We already know from research that 'teacher renewal is enhanced though positive critical real life experiences' (Lauriala 1997, p. 278). Certificated programmes are being developed (for example, at the University of York, where students from many different disciplines will soon have the opportunity to engage with community groups as part of their work for the 'York Award').

The above issue, relating as it does to personal involvement in practical work in the school and beyond, is potentially the more controversial of the two discussed here (although, of course, because politics is always present when any group meets there is no logical reason for this to be so). However, the second issue is perhaps, in real terms, more difficult. It is necessary to determine beyond basic involvement in action what is meant by appropriate citizenship education. What do we expect young people to learn? How can that be assessed and what are the most effective ways to report it? There is a need to make clear the nature of the procedural concepts inherent in citizenship education. Procedural concepts are those which, more so than substantive concepts, characterize the nature of a field of study. Whereas a substantive concept in history might be revolution, a relevant procedural concept (i.e. what one must actually do to understand the past) might be causation. Each procedural concept will have a series of levels contained within it. It may be possible to create a hierarchy of those levels based on an understanding of the combinations of content, contexts, skills and types of explanation which make work harder or easier. At the moment there is very little understanding of what constitutes successful achievement in relation to the procedural concepts of citizenship. There is of course even less understanding of the ways in which skilful teaching can be portrayed. Evaluation of the assessment practices of teachers is understood only very superficially. This is a tremendously difficult area and we have no straightforward answers to give. But we must move away from a situation in which there is greater willingness to focus on the 'old chestnut' of something like bias or the so-called unexciting nature of citizenship than to face clearly more valid and more challenging issues.

CONCLUSION

Citizenship education simply will not happen in any valid form if there is not sustained and serious attention given to teacher education. The area is so important because there is at the moment both large amounts of goodwill from teachers and potential for action, but at the same time there is a tremendously difficult set of challenges to overcome. If we consider the latter first we can see all too easily the negative recent history of teacher education and the great complexity of promoting an appropriate and worthwhile professional development programme. And yet, our data do show that teachers are hugely concerned to care professionally for their students as citizens. Promoters of citizenship education push, at least as far as social and moral responsibility is concerned, at an open door. If citizenship is to mean anything – and in a country which still draws pride from having the aspirations of a liberal democracy, it should – teacher education is a fundamental part of the reform process.

8   Conclusions

This chapter will reflect on issues relevant to the setting up of programmes of citizenship. It will be suggested that only by giving and maintaining a guaranteed place in the National Curriculum for civic education will its present highly marginal role in the life of the school be transformed. The necessary corollary of enjoying such a status is the recognition that any programme of citizenship education on offer must be a determinate programme, spelling out in considerable detail what is expected in the name of citizenship education. Allied to this requirement of determinacy should be a requirement of realism in terms of what reasonably can be expected of schools generally and, more particularly, of education for citizenship within the context of a democracy. There will be some final sceptical remarks as to whether, given the present climate of our politics and the highly interventionist role being played by central government in the nation's schooling, it is likely that citizenship education will be given the place, and allowed to play the role, its apologists would have for it.

The evidence suggests that teachers are well disposed towards citizenship education. As reported by Fogelman (1991; 1997), 43 per cent of primary schools and 62 per cent of secondary schools said that citizenship education is an essential or very important part of the school curriculum. Correspondingly, relatively few schools of either kind said they were not addressing citizenship education at all. Despite this perception of the importance of education for citizenship, there is a welter of evidence suggesting that, for a variety of reasons, citizenship education is a highly marginal curricular concern. In so far as it is being pursued at all, it is as a cross-curricular theme very much in line with the suggestions contained within the National Curriculum Council's (NCC 1990) *Education for Citizenship: Curriculum Guidance 8*. Factors frequently mentioned as discouraging citizenship education are uncertainty as to what it is, lack of adequate resourcing and lack of staff expertise. But pre-eminent among the reasons given is, unsurprisingly, the priority given to the National Curriculum subjects, the teaching of which is a statutory obligation. A common opinion is that it is the pressures on the timetable arising from meeting the demands of the National Curriculum that provides an obstacle to more citizenship education (Fogelman 1997; QCA 1998, pp. 14–17). In the present context of regular inspections and of the publication of school league tables demonstrating how well schools are delivering on government expectations at Key Stages 1, 2 and 3 as well as in the matter of GCSE and A level results, it is no surprise that schools are strongly tempted to confine their activities to those things to which central government clearly attaches the most significance. The identification of the success of a school, with its levels of achievement as revealed in the league tables, compound this tendency. The fear that parents will prefer to send their child to somewhere that appears to be more successful is simply more encouragement to schools to concentrate on the basics and the compulsory. There can be little doubt that as a cross-curricular theme, education for citizenship is at the very margin of most schools' curricular concerns.

If the politicians wish to see education for citizenship seriously pursued within the schools, it must be entrenched within the National Curriculum as a statutory entitlement of every child. The present climate within our schools almost guarantees that, failing such a step, citizenship education will be honoured more in the breach than in the observance, will be more spoken about than actually delivered. No single action could more demonstrate the seriousness of government intent in respect of the enhancement of citizenship than granting to citizenship education a place on the National Curriculum when it comes up for review in the year 2000. It would be the clearest demonstration of a commitment at the highest level to the enhancement of our democratic politics.

Having willed the end (citizenship education), government then needs to will the means. We suggest that what we call a determinate programme of citizenship education be put in place. Such a programme would make plain just what the key concepts are informing such a programme and around which it would be structured and which it is hoped students in our schools will come to utilize in their dealings with their fellow citizens. It would spell out those values and dispositions that must be encouraged and delivered if the aspirations informing a programme of civic education are to stand any chance of realization. It would itemize a range of cognitive skills and aptitudes that must be in place if an active and effective engagement in our public life is going to be a possibility. And last, and by no means least, it must offer a list of the kinds of knowledge and understanding which will afford putative citizens an insight into the nature of the public world into which they are being encouraged to enter as participating members. In keeping with the aspirations of education for citizenship in a democracy it would, while offering teachers guidance, grant to them a measure of the autonomy that civic education is designed to promote within the population at large. However, a statutory document on citizenship education as tightly prescribed as the present Statutory Instruments on English, mathematics and science would be an irony too many.

Within our political tradition, the inspiration behind the clamour for an appropriate civic education is the sense that encouraging and promoting citizenship as an educational end is a recognition of our commitment to a principle of equality. As citizens we are all equal, irrespective of the components of our individual lives (Rawls 1993, p. 79 *et seq.*). Whatever our social status, our gender, our 'race', our ethnicity, our enjoyments of material goods, as citizens we are equal. Our very equality demands that all of us should have the same opportunity to enjoy the benefits of citizenship. At the level of principle, this supports the idea of a citizenship education that is everyone's entitlement. A common programme of education for citizenship would have the additional merit of helping to remove teacher uncertainty about what is being demanded of them in the name of civic education.

The foregoing remarks are very general. That there should be a determinate programme of citizenship education is to say nothing about how such a programme is best generated, or anything about its nature or what reasonably might be expected of it. Part of the confusion surrounding citizenship discourse is its often remarked upon 'essential contestedness' (Gallie 1964, pp. 157–91). Any programme designed to encourage citizenship is going to attract controversy. It is not possible to characterize a conception of citizenship without giving expression to some vision of the kind of society that those designing the programme believe is the best on offer and within which people may best flourish. A programme of citizenship within the context of fascism is going to be a very different kind of creature from one inspired by democratic ideals of a participatory nature. A programme of citizenship for a totalitarian communist regime would have significantly different ambitions from one inspired by Islamic ideals. And, even within a democratic tradition, it is only to be expected that programmes of citizenship will reflect something of the contestedness that is the debate surrounding the nature of democracy. The last point is important if only because some might be tempted to flatly deny that fascism and communism *can* have citizens, simply by virtue of being the kinds of societies they are. Even if one were persuaded by such a definitional stop (Hart 1968, pp. 5–6), it still remains the case that within contexts ostensibly influenced by democratic ideals, the essentially contested nature of democracy should preclude us from being sanguine about the possibility of generating a programme of civic education to which all calling themselves democrats in good faith could sign up.

If there is going to be a programme of citizenship education for our schools, someone has to be given the responsibility for putting it in place. It is unrealistic to expect that, in the present climate of extensive government involvement in our education system, central government will not want to have a say in how the programme is generated and to be comfortable with its recommendations. Whether this is a matter for alarm will depend upon the government's own commitment to the encouragement of a more involved, better informed democratic citizenry. It seems certain that any statutory document on citizenship education will necessitate the minister seeking advice from some advisory body. In this regard it seems likely that some body like the recent Crick Committee will be involved in the drawing up of any such programme.

We must expect that any programme of citizenship education on offer will be rooted in the liberal, pluralistic, democratic tradition. It will, in the manner of the Crick Report (QCA 1998), lay emphasis upon certain key concepts, values and dispositions, and skills and aptitudes which are thought to be particularly valuable in the effective functioning of such a society. In addition, it will list those areas of knowledge and understanding the possession of which will better allow citizens to make a more informed input to the political process.

Whatever the contribution of individual teachers or groups representing teachers to the process of drawing up a programme of education for citizenship, there is no reason to suppose that teachers *qua* teachers should have a privileged say in determining what is going to count as citizenship education. In respect of our own research into teacher attitudes towards good citizenship, the fact that tolerance of diversity and respect for the views of others and an emphasis upon the importance of participation within the community loom so large may transpire to be important for the prospects of having a teaching force well disposed to the recommendations contained within a programme of education for citizenship. But such findings should in no way be granted special standing in the deliberations of a group drawing up a programme of civic education. As in the way there is no reason to suppose that only judges have a particular insight into the nature of law, only mathematicians into mathematics or only scientists into science, so with teachers in respect of citizenship education. Indeed, in one crucial respect, typically teachers are at a disadvantage as compared with other groups: law is at the very heart of a judge's work, as mathematics and science are at the heart of mathematics and science teaching. For the overwhelming preponderance of teachers, however, citizenship education barely figures as a significant curricular concern. The task of understanding the various desiderata that define what it is to be an effective, active, engaged democratic citizen within the kind of society we are is, in large measure, a philosophical task. It is best carried out by those who by training and education, interest and commitment, have thought hard about the nature of our democracy. In this task, they will consult interested parties and informed opinion. Within this context, the teacher voice can and should be heard.

If we are planning *de novo* a programme of citizenship education for all children between the ages 5–16, there is an explicit need to consider the principles informing the programme, the values finding expression within the programme, the set of characteristics a successful product of such a programme would exhibit and, very importantly, the determinate learning outcomes that would allow us to make better grounded judgements about how successful the delivery of the programme had been. In our context, this will certainly entail a detailed and fundamental examination of the nature of our democracy and its perceived adequacies and inadequacies, plus an exploration of the dispositions and attitudes necessary within the populace to enhance our democratic processes and an articulation of the knowledge and understandings necessary to being a competent and well-informed participant within the democratic debate. None of this precludes individual teachers with a particular interest in the relevant concerns from being consulted or making a contribution to the discussion. None of this precludes due recognition being given to teachers as a group by their becoming members of the committee charged with determining a programme of citizenship education. It would be useful to have the professional voice stating what realistically might be expected of children at the different key stages, and schools, in the delivery of such a programme. However, to reiterate, it is not the case that – simply because the data suggests that in the minds of the majority of teachers this or that set of opinions characterize citizenship – more teacher sentiment should be reflected within a programme of civic education. The determination of ideals is never to be settled by reference to preponderant opinion – if, of course, such exists.

Those charged with the task of drawing up a programme of civic education will have to craft and sculpt a programme of citizenship education giving expression to *choices* that promote *some* key concepts rather than others, place particular emphasis upon *some* values and dispositions rather than others, seek to engender *some* skills and aptitudes above others, and make key decisions about what knowledge and understanding a programme of civic education promotes. It is not to be expected that any programme on offer will enjoy the unanimous support of all of those who would see themselves as the heirs to, and products of, a liberal, pluralistic and democratic society.

A programme inspired by the ideals of liberal, pluralistic democracy is only what it is: it is not something else. A liberal programme of citizenship education is not a feminist programme of education for citizenship, is not a programme of civic education actuated by a concern for citizenship in the post-modern world. A given programme inspired by liberal ideals is not even one that necessarily pleases all liberals. Programmes of civic education that are too ambitious, too far reaching in the range of wrongs they wish to put to right, are doomed to disappointment. To try and do too much in the name of citizenship education is to exacerbate the already too familiar confusion surrounding citizenship education, its point and purposes. We make a plea that any putative programme of civic education appropriate to a liberal, pluralistic, democratic society has aspirations that feasibly schools can realize. The one element that typically defines the debate surrounding education for citizenship in our society is the hope that the quality of our democratic debate can be enhanced. Whether the form of democracy espoused is representative or participatory (or is one of the variants along the spectrum), the common lament is that too few participate in democratic politics. At either the national or local level, the feeling is that too few vote. And this lack of interest is mirrored at the emerging European level. The wealth of evidence suggesting that young people in particular are apathetic about, even contemptuous of, traditional politics and politicians simply confirms the belief that something needs to be done to encourage a more active engagement in public affairs. It is therefore little surprise that those believing in democracy as something to be treasured (though often for very different reasons) (Harrison 1993) hope that through education and schooling the prospects of democratic politics can be transformed.

The successful implementation of such a programme would result in citizens altogether more confident of their ability to participate in and shape the conduct of public affairs. From the perspective of pupils, schools will empower them to engage effectively in society as informed, active, critical and responsible participants in public matters. From the perspective of society, an active and politically literate citizenry will be persuaded that they can influence government and community affairs at any level. The ideal citizen in a democratic context is an individual aware of his or her rights and responsibilities, sufficiently empowered to enjoy and exercise their entitlements and who, being conscious of their responsibilities towards others, meets them. Such an individual is someone who understands social interaction in terms of certain key concepts (tolerance, the rule of law, etc.) who has internalized relevant values and dispositions (concern for the common good, empathy with others, etc.), is possessed of a repertoire of skills and aptitudes (ability to express a coherent point of view, ability to detect bias, etc.) and has that knowledge and insight that allow for a more sophisticated understanding of issues in the public domain. Citizenship education is about promoting and encouraging just such individuals. In short, citizenship education is about encouraging a sense of belonging to a society as well as empowering individuals to enjoy their entitlements, giving them rights as members of a society while at the same time encouraging in them a recognition of the obligations that each citizen incurs in respect of every other citizen. If successful, we would have a more participative and better informed democracy, a more active citizenry pursuing in the name of the common good a whole range of community (generously interpreted) involvements, while extending to everyone else a proper regard premised on a proper understanding and tolerance of their separateness as persons and as members of sub-groups (cultural, ethnic and religious). This is the theory.

It is a standard criticism of liberal theory that the realization of the ideals for which it stands is doomed to disappointment (Faulks 1998). It systematically disregards all those deeply entrenched structural features of our society that militate against so many individuals enjoying to any real degree those entitlements that liberal society exists to promote and guarantee. In disregarding the gendered and racist nature of our society, the gross inequalities in income, educational opportunity and the like, liberal theory fails to take seriously those elements that limit the ability of so many individuals to shape their own lives, pursue fruitfully their life plans and have an influence on the decision-making processes within our democratic polity. In such a society, for too many, talk of the substantive enjoyment of rights and the equality of the citizen rings hollow. There is much in this that is clearly correct. We are only too familiar with the fact that the different life circumstances into which people are born have a profound and lasting impact on their life opportunities. We are only too aware of the institutionalized ways in which 'race', ethnicity and gender play a key role in denying to whole groups of people access to the opportunities and benefits that differently situated groups in society enjoy.

There is much to be done at the social and political level to rectify such palpable injustices. There exists the belief that education might play its part in alleviating some of them. There are all kinds of concerns arising out of the ethnic diversity now typifying our society, which gives rise to whole ethnic groupings feeling themselves to be at the margins of society.

What are the implications of these surely indisputable statements? We leave to one side the issue of their being a critique of liberalism. It is at this stage that a plea for realism seems to be necessary. We need to recognize that, whatever the common humane impulse that inspires them, citizenship education is not anti-sexist education, is not anti-racist education, is not multicultural education, is not PSE, is not values education, is not environmental education, is not global education, is not even human rights education. The substantive concerns defining any likely programme of citizenship education in our society are not those. There are no doubt all kinds of linkages (conceptual and more substantial) that might be made between possible citizenship education programmes and other humanely inspired programmes of education. But they are not the same and any effort to load education for citizenship with their driving ambitions will be to the detriment of a realistically grounded programme inspired by the thought of enhancing the quality of our democratic life. The task of citizenship education in our society is to promote and encourage individuals with the wherewithal to better play a part in our democracy. If it is successful in putting into place a programme of learning that realizes its ambitions, it will have achieved what it set out to achieve. If, inspired by its demands, we have a teaching force better trained and equipped to play its role in civic education (see Chapter 7), and if schools – recognizing the demands laid upon them by civic education's new status as a pupil's entitlement – review their structures and practices (see Chapter 6), we have reason to suppose that in encouraging (as we clearly can do) a new and more sustained democratic discourse within our schools, individuals will reap the benefits. We know from our research that teachers overwhelmingly feel that much of what any likely programme of civic education is going to recognize as constitutive of the requirements of a citizen infused by democratic values is at the heart of what it is to be a good citizen. Teachers, as a group, are committed to the promotion of tolerance of the views of others, the development of critical thinking, the encouragement of a recognition of our obligations to others and a preparedness to discharge our obligations. We know that, characteristically, teachers believe citizenship education to be important and would like to give it a larger role in the life of the school. However, diluting a programme of education for citizenship in pursuit of other hugely important goals is to the detriment of civic education and will not be helpful in achieving the other goals either.

But, if schools are successful in producing citizens along the lines of (for example) a Crick Report-inspired programme of citizenship education, we can say, at least, the following with confidence. If pupils are equipped with key concepts like fairness, justice, the rule of law and, having those values and dispositions, and skills and aptitudes seen as crucial to meeting and discharging responsibilities as a citizen in a democracy, the possibility (though not the guarantee) exists that they will try and play their part as democratic citizens. And because they are equipped with the skills and characteristics a successful programme of citizenship has inculcated, it is more possible than it might have been before that, in their individual dealings with all those who the deep structures of our society have disadvantaged, they will confront them as individuals and not as stereotypical blacks or women or members of an ethnic minority. We should not underestimate the beneficial 'carry over' from one area to another and by this, at the individual level anyway, prejudice and arbitrariness in human affairs will be to some extent diminished. This can only be a good thing.

The great dilemma permeating this whole area of debate is whether such deeply entrenched features of society as racism and sexism are amenable to the effect of individual actions. Can we eliminate or alleviate the impact of these factors in our social life by shaping individual consciousness and creating dispositions to act through devising mass programmes of education devoted to their extirpation? Perhaps the only thing that can be said with confidence here is that efforts made at the individual level via education to alert individuals to the irrational nature of racism and sexism (to take the easiest examples to indict as irrational) surely do have an impact on the quality of individual relationships existing between those who regard the sex or colour of a person's skin as being irrelevant and those who are the victims of such prejudices.

There is, of course, no guarantee that a citizenry more eager to participate in political activity, and with the critical tools to scrutinize more adequately what is going on and being done in their name, will not find that the democratic structures which are in place militate against their effective participation. Again, the only thing that can be said with confidence is that the louder and more coherent are the voices complaining at this failure of democracy, the greater is the possibility that changes will be made. It may or may not be a criticism of liberalism that its approach to those who are citizens is too a-historical, not sufficiently socially embedded. But it is to mis-construe a liberal programme of citizenship education to complain it is not addressing directly just those features of our society that do detract from the full enjoyment for far too many of the rights and entitlements which liberal theory celebrates. Its limited end is to put citizens in a position to more effectively and actively pursue their rights and entitlements. It seeks to remind them of the obligations we have to others who, as citizens them-selves, have rights and entitlements and correlative claims upon us as they follow their preferred lives. To that end, it encourages tolerance, empathy and sympathy, respect for other traditions, and the disposition to participate in their own communities. If successful, the incidental ramifications in respect of racism and sexism can be considerable – certainly at the level of according individuals respect irrespective of race or gender. But, it is as well to remind ourselves, nothing is guaranteed. In education, to adopt the adage, we travel hopefully. It is still open to anyone to either reject what is on offer or, having mastered it, turn his or her back on what reason and decency stand for.

Racism and sexism are great social evils. We cannot simply accept their presence in our society as inevitable features of our life. While not being so optimistic as to imagine they can be wholly banished, it is incumbent upon us to strive to diminish their impact on individual lives. The way forward is surely to advance on all levels: create appropriate educational programmes that take as their primary purpose the undermining of racism's and sexism's hold upon too many people, plus programmes of political action that tackle them and their manifestations directly. There must be some scepticism as to whether, even if anti-racist and anti-sexist programmes of education are successful in raising levels of individual consciousness about such evils, they will be put to flight. In the same way as citizenship education can promote at the individual level more decent dealings one with the other, so anti-racist and anti-sexist programmes of education can encourage raised awareness and understanding of the relevant issues. But whether this is suffi-cient to remove the pervasive ramifications of sexism and racism must be doubted. To improve job opportunities, to extend educational opportunities, to give substance to the idea of equality before the law and so on seems to demand action of a quite different kind, action taken at the highest political level as an expression of the determination not to tolerate such blights upon our social life. And, going back to civic education, programmes of education for citizenship that genuinely enhance the requisite democratic skills, values and dispositions of our citizenry have their part to play (incidentally as it were) in pressurizing government to take action and pass laws that will go some way to tackling the endemic racism and sexism of our society. Citizenship education does this by being clear as to its primary and overriding purpose.

At the time of writing, the United Kingdom is in the throes of a constitutional ferment: devolution in Wales and Scotland, new forms of voting seriously being mooted and problematic issues to do with our relationship to Europe. There is much talk of overlapping citizenships culminating in the rhetoric of citizen of the world. As our society becomes increasingly multi-ethnic, there are perceived to be problems of forging a common identity under which all of us can shelter. Whether programmes of citizenship education along the lines mooted in this book can aid much in the forging of such a common identity and generation of overlapping citizenships is another area for study. Whether the commonly shared commitments to democracy and the desire to be an effective democratic citizen are 'thick' enough commitments (Kymlicka 1995) to bind diverse groupings so that they can share a common identity must be open to doubt. In the case of overlapping citizenries, the situation is also a matter for debate. The same key concepts, values and dispositions, skills and attitudes, and suitably modified knowledge and understanding might equip a 'European citizen' to participate in the democratic politics of the European Community. What seems so problematic is how far the desire to participate in European politics is dependent not just on possessing the wherewithal necessary to participate but on possessing a sense of European identity. Again, the issue of forging such an identity seems relevant to the actual enjoyment of European entitlements as against enjoying citizenship in name only. In respect of global citizenship, the situation is altogether more murky. All of the anchorage points which are normally those informing citizenship discourse (a determinate territory, legal and political systems operative within a given territory, a government protecting rights and entitlements and the like) are largely absent. The fear must be that we have here an instance of what Wittgenstein calls 'language idling'. Whatever, at the present stage, talk of being a citizen of the world connotes, it is so far removed from the ordinary context of citizenship discourse to that it seems that such talk represents nothing more than a desire to get us to recognize that even in the most distant climes, 'they' are more like 'us' than sometimes we remember. It is an effort to extend our sympathies beyond our more immediate confines – an example of Rorty's 'sentimental education' (Rorty 1998, p. 167 *et seq.*). We rejected the standard critique of liberalism as being too a-social and a-historical in its approach and in its characterization of the agents who act within the political and social world as not being relevant to liberal theories of civic education. However, the communitarian critique might well be more meaningful in respect of any ambitions liberal programmes of citizenship education also have to forge a sense of belonging as a precondition to being a democratic citizen committed to something other than the pursuit of his or her own private ends. The notion of a common good seems altogether to be more of a motivating factor in democratic discourse if there exists a genuine sense of sharing and belonging to a polity. The discussion of these issues, which go to the very heart of much contemporary political theorizing, must await another occasion – except to say that whether individuals and groups feel they belong is surely a function of how they perceive themselves to be viewed by society and others. No number of educational programmes can engender a sense that individuals count unless there is palpable evidence that they do. Evidence that they count has to take the form of taking seriously their interests, hopes, fears, life projects and commitments. Partialities and attachments grow out of a shared common life. Discrimination, in all of its guises, goes against the very possibility of forging a common identity and of generating a sense of belonging at any level of social life.

This book has contained a wealth of detailed suggestions on how schools charged with delivering a democratically inspired programme of citizenship education should meet the challenge. The theme informing these suggestions is that schools will not deliver unless both teachers and students are regarded as citizens. To this end, sustained, and often uncomfortable, thought must be given to not only the formal curricular elements that define the programme but also to the very structures and practices that constitute the life of the school. We suggest, consonant with the ambitions of civic education for a democracy, a searching review of the life of the school. The values finding expression in the push for democratic citizenship should be reflected throughout the very fabric of school life. Pupil–pupil relationships, teacher–teacher relationships and, absolutely fundamentally, teacher–pupil relationships should, as far as possible, be permeated by democratic ideals. In short, the recommendation is that schools had better practise what they preach. We hope that citizenship education will find itself at the very heart of the curriculum. It is plain that democratic politics is not what it could be. It is plain that too much of our social life is not sufficiently influenced by the ideals of tolerance, mutual respect, acceptance of difference, respect for the law, a preparedness to do as much for our community as we might, or by a concern for reason. Civic education seeks to further all such ideals in the name of enhancing our democracy. The teachers in our research have a strong sense of the importance of the ideals just outlined. Where they need guidance is in embracing the more ostensibly political dimension of democratic citizenship. What the Crick Report calls 'political literacy' directs attention in that direction. And it must be true that, if citizens wish to have some influence on decisions taken at the national level or beyond, they need to be informed on all matters relevant to the taking of such decisions. Schools with suitably informed and qualified teachers could aid in just this task.

Our great anxiety is whether central government will deliver on its oft-repeated enthusiasm for citizenship education. Speculation is probably fruitless. Government will, after all, simply do what it wants. There is fierce competition for the allotment of time that citizenship education as a statutory entitlement might expect. Many of the candidates will not have as their primary purpose the encouragement of critical debate and reflection that citizenship education exists to promote. Recently, central government has been shown to be increasingly impatient with those who do not want to be participants in the agenda which it has laid down. And nowhere has the displeasing certainty that has infected government in recent times been more evident than in education. Successive governments have discouraged any serious debate about education, its aims and purposes. They have exhibited a dispiriting certainty that they know what is best and how it is schools can be improved. This has inevitably involved a disregard of the teacher voice. It is very difficult to view teachers, within the present dispensation, as other than servants of the state delivering what their political masters demand. None of this is finally incompatible with central government giving the go-ahead to citizenship education as part of the National Curriculum. But it would not be in character with the recent temper of government ambitions in education (and elsewhere) to promote a course of study whose outcomes are quite so unpredictable. Unless teachers and pupils are given, compatible with the nature of democratic politics, the freedom to pursue issues wherever they may go, citizenship education will be undermined from the very start.

Appendix
Citizenship Questionnaire (Form AGB)

This survey is being conducted in an effort to collect and assess data regarding views of good citizenship. The information you provide will help determine what role citizenship education should play in the school curriculum and how it should be taught. Your answers will be confidential. There are no right or wrong answers.

BACKGROUND INFORMATION: Place an 'X' in the space that best describes you.

Ethnic Group (this listing represents official Department for Education categories)

☐ White   ☐ Indian   ☐ Chinese   ☐ Other _____
☐ Black Caribbean   ☐ Pakistani   ☐ Asian   ☐ Information
☐ Black African   ☐ Bangladeshi   Refused
☐ Black (Other)

Gender

☐ Male   ☐ Female

Age

☐ 20–30 years   ☐ 31–40 years   ☐ 41–50 years   ☐ 51–60 years
☐ over 60 years

Age Group Currently Taught

_____

Route to Teaching Certificate

☐ Initial Teacher Training (3 Year Teacher College)
☐ Fourth Year BA Degree
☐ Three Years at University/Main Subject Speciality/PGCE
☐ Other _____

Total Years of Teaching Experience
☐ 1–5 years ☐ 6–10 years ☐ 11–15 years ☐ 16–20 years
☐ over 20 years

CITIZENSHIP QUESTIONS

For each response on the questionnaire, you will be asked to place an 'X' on a line. The far left end of the line represents **strong agreement (SA)** with the statement, while the far right end of the line represents **strong disagreement (SD)**. You may place an 'X' any place on the line to show the extent to which you agree or disagree with a statement. If your feelings are neutral, the mark would be near the centre.

The following characteristics are important qualities of a good citizen:

	SA				SD
• knowledge of current events	—	—	—	—	— —
• participation in community or school affairs	—	—	—	—	— —
• acceptance of an assigned responsibility	—	—	—	—	— —
• concern for the welfare of others	—	—	—	—	— —
• moral and ethical behaviour	—	—	—	—	— —
• acceptance of authority of those in supervisory roles	—	—	—	—	— —
• ability to question ideas	—	—	—	—	— —
• ability to make wise decisions	—	—	—	—	— —
• knowledge of government	—	—	—	—	— —
• patriotism	—	—	—	—	— —
• fulfilment of family responsibilities	—	—	—	—	— —
• knowledge of world community	—	—	—	—	— —
• tolerance of diversity within society	—	—	—	—	— —

The following have influenced <u>my</u> citizenship:

	SA				SD
• parents	—	—	—	—	— —
• friends	—	—	—	—	— —
• brothers and/or sisters	—	—	—	—	— —
• religious leaders	—	—	—	—	— —
• television and/or films	—	—	—	—	— —
• grandparents and/or other relatives	—	—	—	—	— —
• guardians	—	—	—	—	— —
• teachers	—	—	—	—	— —
• head teachers or other school officials	—	—	—	—	— —
• extra-curricular activities	—	—	—	—	— —

- other students   —   —   —   —   —   —
- youth leaders   —   —   —   —   —   —

I believe the following are a <u>threat</u> to a child's citizenship:

	SA					SD
television and/or films	—	—	—	—	—	—
drugs and/or alcohol	—	—	—	—	—	—
peer pressure	—	—	—	—	—	—
sexual activity	—	—	—	—	—	—
negative role models	—	—	—	—	—	—
family conflict	—	—	—	—	—	—
school environment	—	—	—	—	—	—
excessive leisure time	—	—	—	—	—	—
unearned material rewards	—	—	—	—	—	—
community environment	—	—	—	—	—	—

I believe that the following classroom activity(ies) <u>would be</u> helpful in developing a child's citizenship:

	SA					SD
an activity in which the child learns about the traditions and values that shaped his/her community and country	—	—	—	—	—	—
an activity dealing with current events	—	—	—	—	—	—
an activity in which the child learns about the history and government of his/her country	—	—	—	—	—	—
an activity in which the child works on a community project with community leaders	—	—	—	—	—	—
a problem solving activity	—	—	—	—	—	—
an activity using constitutional and legal processes	—	—	—	—	—	—
an activity that aims at the child's individual needs and interests	—	—	—	—	—	—
an activity in which the child looks at worldwide needs and responsibilities	—	—	—	—	—	—

References

Addis, I. (1992) *What Can the Matter Be?* London, David Fulton.

Ahier, J. and Ross, A. (1995) *The Social Subjects within the Curriculum: children's social learning in the National Curriculum.* London, Falmer Press.

Appleby, J., Hunt, L. and Jacob, M. (1994) *Telling the Truth about History.* London, Norton.

Aristotle (1967) *Politics* (Jowett, B. trans). New York, Random House.

Austin, R. (1995) Using Electronic Mail in Initial Teacher Education to Develop European Awareness. *Journal of Information Technology for Teacher Education,* 4, 2, 227–35.

Baglin Jones, E. and Jones, N. (1992) *Education for Citizenship: ideas and perspectives for cross-curricular study.* London, Kogan Page.

Ball, S. (1994) *Education Reform: a critical and post-structuralist approach.* Buckingham, Open University Press.

Ball, W. (1997) Using the Internet to Enhance Classroom and Citizenship Information, in Reeher, G. and Cammarano, J. (eds) *Education for Citizenship: ideas and innovations in political learning.* Oxford, Rowman & Littlefield.

Barber, M. (1997) *The Learning Game: arguments for an education revolution.* London, Indigo.

Batho, G. (1990) The History of the Teaching of Civics and Citizenship in English Schools. *The Curriculum Journal,* 1, 1, 91–100.

Bennell, S. J., Daniel, P. and Hughes, C. E. (1996) Partnership in Action: bringing central America into the primary curriculum, in Steiner, M. (ed.) *Developing the Global Teacher: theory and practice in initial teacher education.* Stoke on Trent, Trentham Books.

Blair, T. (1995) End the Take and Give Away Society. *The Guardian,* 23 March.

Board of Education (1928) *Report of the Consultative Committee on Secondary Education with Special Reference to Grammar Schools and Technical High Schools* (The Spens Report). London, HMSO.

Board of Education (1943) *Curriculum and Examinations in Secondary Schools: Report of the Committee of the Secondary Schools Examinations Council* (The Norwood Report). London, HMSO.

Borg, W. R. and Gall, M. D. (1989) *Educational Research* (5th edn). New York, Longman.

References

Brennan, T. (1981) *Political Education and Democracy*. Cambridge, Cambridge University Press.

Brown, K. and Brown, M. (1996) A More Rounded Education: global perspectives in modern languages and initial teacher education, in Steiner, M. (ed.) *Developing the Global Teacher: theory and practice in initial teacher education*. Stoke on Trent, Trentham Books.

Bryson, V. (1993) Feminism, in Eatwell, R. and Wright, A. (eds) *Contemporary Political Ideologies*. London, Pinter Publishers.

Campbell, R. and Davies, I. (1995) Education and Green Citizenship: an exploratory study with student teachers. *Journal of Further and Higher Education*, 19, 3, 20–31.

Canfield, K. P. (1997) The Internet as a Tool for Student Citizenship, in Reeher, G. and Cammarano, J. (eds) *Education for Citizenship: ideas and innovations in political learning*. Oxford, Rowman & Littlefield.

Carr, W. (1991) Education for Citizenship. *British Journal of Educational Studies*, 39, 4, 373–85.

Cherlin, A. J., Chase-Lansdale, P. L. and McRae, C. (1998) Effects of Parental Divorce on Mental Health throughout the Life Course. *American Sociological Review*, 63, 239–49.

Children's Society (no date) *Education for Citizenship*. London, The Children's Society.

Chitty, C. and Benn, C. (1996) *Thirty Years On: is comprehensive education alive and well or struggling to survive?* London, David Fulton.

Clarke, K. (1992) *Speech for the North of England Education Conference*. Delivered on 4 January at Southport. London, DES.

Cogan, J. J. and Derricott, R. (eds) (1998) *Citizenship for the Twenty-first Century: an international perspective on education*. London, Kogan Page.

Cole, M. (1942) *Education for Democracy*. London, Allen & Unwin.

Commission on Citizenship (1990) *Encouraging Citizenship*. London, HMSO.

Conley, F. (1991) *Political Understanding across The Curriculum*. Manchester, The Politics Association.

Connell, R. W. (1971) *The Child's Construction of Politics*. London, Melbourne University Press.

Convery, A., Evans, M., Green, S., Macaro, E. and Mellor, J. (1997) *Pupils' Perceptions of Europe: identity and education*. London, Cassell.

Council for Education in World Citizenship (1997) *Towards Citizenship Support Pack: materials to support a programme of education for citizenship for 14–19-year-olds*. London, CEWC.

Crawford, K. (1996) Neo-Conservative Perspectives on Culture and Nationhood and their Impact upon the School Curriculum in England and Wales. *Children's Social and Economics Education*, 1, 3, 208–22.

Crewe, I., Searing, D. and Connover, P. (1996) Citizenship: the revival of an idea, in *Citizenship and Civic Education*. London, The Citizenship Foundation.

Crick, B. and Porter, A. (eds) (1978) *Political Education and Political Literacy*. London, Longman.

Cunningham, J. (1992) Rights, Responsibilities and School Ethos, in Baglin Jones, E. and Jones, N. (eds) *Education for Citizenship: ideas and perspectives for cross-curricular study*. London, Kogan Page.

Davies, I. (1992) Guidelines for Political Education. Unpublished D.Phil. thesis, University of York.

Davies, I. (1993a) Teaching Political Understanding in Secondary Schools. *Curriculum*, 14, 3, 163–77.

Davies, I. (1993b) The Reform of Education: how and why are guideline documents produced for teachers and are they of any value? *Curriculum*, 14, 2, 114–24.

Davies, I. (1993c) Confusion and Incoherence in Educational Policy Making, or, Is that Right? *Grassroots*, 63, 1–8. Manchester, The Politics Association.

Davies, I. (1994a) Education for Citizenship. *Curriculum*, 15, 2, 67–76.

Davies, I. (1994b) Whatever Happened to Political Education? *Educational Review*, 46, 1, 29–38.

Davies, I. (1997) Education for European Citizenship: issues in history education. *Evaluation and Research in Education*, 11, 3, 119–28.

Davies, I. and Rey, M. (1998) Questioning Identities: issues for teachers and children, in Holden, C. and Clough, N. (eds) *Children as Citizens: education for participation*. London, Jessica Kingsley Publishers.

Davies, I. and Sobisch, A. (1997) *Developing European Citizens*. Sheffield, Sheffield Hallam University Press.

Davies, I. and Williams, R. (1998) Interpretations of History: history teachers at work. *Teaching History*, 91, 36–40.

Davies, I. Gray, G. and Stephens, P. (1998) Education for Citizenship: a case study of 'Democracy Day' at a comprehensive school. *Educational Review*, 50, 1, 15–27.

Davies, I., Gregory, I. and Riley, S. (1997) *Teachers' Conceptions of Good Citizenship*. Paper presented at the British Educational Research Association, September 1997.

Dawson, R. E., Prewitt, K. and Dawson, K. S. (1977) *Political Socialisation*. Boston, Little, Brown & Co.

DEA (1998) *Training Teachers for Tomorrow*. London, Development Education Association.

de Beer, P. (1998) Tony Blair propose une 'alliance patriotique' aux tories pro-européens. *Le Monde*, 23 January, p. 4.

Deem, R., Brehony, K. and Heath, S. (1995) *Active Citizenship and the Governing of Schools*. Buckingham, Open University Press.

DES (1967) *Towards World History. Pamphlet No. 52*. London, HMSO.

DES (1984) *Initial Teacher Training: approval of courses. Circular No. 3/84*. London, HMSO.

DES (1985) *Education for All. Report of the Commission of Enquiry into the Education of Children from Ethnic Minority Groups* (The Swann Report). London, HMSO.

DES (1989) *Initial Teacher Training: approval of courses. Circular No. 27/89*. London, HMSO.

Dewey, J. (1916/1966) *Democracy and Education*. London, Free Press/Macmillan.

DfEE (1998) *Teaching: High Status, High Standards. Requirements for Courses of Initial Teacher Training*. London, DfEE.

Dunkin, M. J., Welch, A., Merritt, A., Phillips, R. and Craven, R. (1998) Teachers' Explanations of Classroom Events: knowledge and beliefs about teaching civics and citizenship. *Teaching and Teacher Education*, 14, 2, 141–51.

Dynneson, T. L. (1992) What Does Good Citizenship Mean to Students? *Social Education*, 56, 1, 55–8.

Dynneson, T. L., Gross, R. E. and Nickel, J. A. (1987) *An Exploratory Survey of*

References

CUFA Members' Opinions and Practices Pertaining to Citizenship Education in Social Studies, 1985–86. Stanford, CA, Center for Educational Research at Stanford, 88-CERAS-18.

Edwards, J. (1993) Cross-curricular Theme Pack 1: Citizenship. Centre for Citizenship Studies in Education, University of Leicester.

Elliott, J. (1993) Reconstructing Teacher Education. London, Falmer Press.

Entwistle, H. (1973) Towards an Educational Theory of Political Socialisation. Paper read at the Philosophy of Education Society conference, New Orleans, USA, 15 April.

Etzioni, A. (1995) The Spirit of Community: rights, responsibilities and the communitarian agenda. London, Fontana.

Evans, D., Gräßler, H. and Pouwels, J. (eds) (1997) Human Rights and Values Education in Europe: research in educational law, curricula and textbooks. Freiburg, Fillibach-Verl.

Evans, R. (1997) In Defence of History. London, Granta Books.

Exploring Citizenship Pack (no date) Exploring Citizenship: a schools pack on the use and provision of public services. Leicester, Leicester University.

Faulks, K. (1998) Citizenship in Modern Britain. Edinburgh, Edinburgh University Press.

Federal Trust (1998) Practising Citizenship: organizing a mock European election. London, Federal Trust.

Fogelman, K. (ed.) (1991) Citizenship in Schools. London, David Fulton.

Fogelman, K. (1995) Citizenship Education: European teachers' course. Uppsala, Sweden, October–November 1995. Strasbourg, Council of Europe.

Fogelman, K. (1997) Citizenship Education in England, in Kennedy, K. (1997) Citizenship Education and the Modern State. London, Falmer Press.

Foster, E. (1999) Introduction: the idea of political education. Special Issue on Political Education. Oxford Review of Education, 25, 1, 2, 5–22.

Fouts, J. T. (1995) Concepts of Citizenship: a multi-nation study on the qualities of good citizenship and implications for schools. Unpublished manuscript, Seattle, Seattle Pacific University.

Fouts, J. (1997) The Elusive Concept of Citizenship. Unpublished paper.

Fouts, J. T. (ed.) (forthcoming) The Meaning of Citizenship.

Frankenstein, M. and Powell, A. B. (1994) Towards Liberatory Mathematics: Paulo Freire's epistemology and ethnomathematics, in McLaren, P. L. and Lankshear, C. (eds) Politics of Liberation: paths from Freire. London, Routledge.

Fukuyama, F. (1992) The End of History and the Last Man. London, Hamish Hamilton.

Fukuyama, F. (1997) The End of Order. London, Social Market Foundation.

Gallie, W. B. (1964) Philosophy and the Historical Understanding. London, Chatto & Windus.

Gilbert, R. (1984) The Impotent Image: reflections of ideology in the school curriculum. London, Falmer Press.

Gilbert, R. (1995) Education for Citizenship and the Problem of Identity in Postmodern Political Culture, in Ahier, J. and Ross, A. (eds) The Social Subjects within the Curriculum: children's social learning within the National Curriculum. London, Falmer Press.

Gipps, C. (1993) Policy-making and the Use and Misuse of Evidence, in Chitty, C. and Simon, B. (eds) *Education Answers Back: critical responses to government policy*. London, Lawrence & Wishart.

Gleeson, D. (1987) *TVEI and Secondary Education: a critical approach*. Milton Keynes, Open University Press.

Gohm, C. L., Oishi, S., Darlington, J. and Diener, E. (1998) Culture, Parental Conflict, Parental Marital Status and the Subjective Well-being of Young Adults. *Journal of Marriage and the Family*, 60, 319–34.

Gollancz, V. and Somervell, D. (1914) *Political Education at a Public School*. Collins, London.

Gonzalo, C. and Villanueva, M. (1995) Geography and Multicultural Education: using students' own experiences of migration, in Osler, A., Rathenow, H-F. and Starkey, H. (eds) *Teaching for Citizenship in Europe*. Stoke on Trent, Trentham Books.

Gorman, M. (1994) Education for Citizenship, in Verma, G. K. and Pumfrey, P. D. (eds) *Cross-curricular Contexts, Themes and Dimensions in Primary Schools*. London, Falmer Press.

Gottman, J. M. and Krokoff, L. J. (1998) Marital Interaction and Satisfaction: a longitudinal view. *Journal of Consulting and Clinical Psychology*, 57, 47–52.

Green, C. A. (1987) The Development of Two Survey Instruments Used to Determine the Status of Citizenship Education. Unpublished MA thesis, The University of Texas of the Permian Basin.

Greenstein, F. (1965) *Children and Politics*. London, Yale University Press.

Griffith, R. (1998) *Educational Citizenship and Independent Learning*. London, Jessica Kingsley Publishers.

Gross, R. E. and Dynneson, T. L. (eds) (1991) *Social Science Perspectives on Citizenship Education*. New York and London: Teachers College, Columbia University.

Haigh, G. (1994) Voices of Reason. *The Times Educational Supplement*, 27 May.

Harber, C. (1994) International Political Development and Democratic Teacher Education. *Educational Review*, 46, 2, 159–65.

Harber, C. (1995) *Developing Democratic Education*. Ticknall, Education Now Books.

Harber, C. (1997) *School Effectiveness and Education for Democracy and Non-violence*. Paris, UNESCO.

Harber, C. and Meighan, R. (1986) Democratic Method in Teacher Training for Political Education. *Teaching Politics*, 15, 2, 179–87.

Hargreaves, D. (1972) *Social Relations in a Secondary School*. London, Routledge & Kegan Paul.

Harrison, R. (1993) *Democracy*. London, Routledge.

Hart, H. L. A. (1968) *Punishment and Responsibility*. Oxford, Oxford University Press.

Healey, D. (1990) *The Time of My Life*. London, Penguin.

Heater, D. (1977a) Political Education in Schools: the official attitude, in Crick, B. and Heater, D. *Essays on Political Education*. Lewes, Falmer Press.

Heater, D. (1977b) A Burgeoning of Interest: political education in Britain, in Crick, B. and Heater, D. *Essays on Political Education*. Lewes, Falmer Press.

Heater, D. (1983) The Origins of CEWC (Council for Education in World Citizenship). Paper presented at a seminar in the Department of Educational Studies, University of York.

References

Heater, D. (1984) *Peace Through Education. The Contribution of the Council for Education in World Citizenship.* Lewes, Falmer Press.

Heater, D. (1990) *Citizenship: the civic ideal in world history, politics and education.* London, Longman.

Hicks, D. (1988) *Education for Peace. Issues, Principles and Action in the Classroom.* London, Routledge.

Hicks, D. (1994) *Educating for the Future: a practical classroom guide.* Godalming, World Wide Fund for Nature.

Hicks, D. and Holden, C. (1995) *Visions of the Future.* Stoke on Trent, Trentham Books.

Hoelman, L. and Ester, P. (1994) The Ethos of Individualism in Cross-cultural Perspective: exploring the European values data. Paper presented at the fourth ISEEI Conference, University of Gräz.

Humberside County Council Education Department (undated) *Political and Social Education: guidelines for schools and colleges.* Beverley, Humberside County Council.

Ichilov, O. (ed.) (1998) *Citizenship and Citizenship Education in a Changing World.* London, The Woburn Press.

Inglehart, R. (1996) Generational Shifts in Citizenship Behaviours: the role of education and economic security in the declining respect for authority in industrial society. *Prospects*, 26, 4, 653–62.

Jackson, P. (1968) *Life in Classrooms.* Eastbourne, Holt, Rinehart & Winston.

Jahoda, G. (1963) The Development of Children's Ideas about Country and Nationality. *British Journal of Educational Psychology*, 33, 143–53.

John, P. and Osborne, A. (1992) The Influence of School Ethos on Pupils' Citizenship Attitudes. *Educational Review*, 44, 153–67.

Jowell, R. and Park, A. (1997) Young People, Politics and Citizenship – a Disengaged Generation? Paper presented at the Citizenship Foundation Annual Colloquium. London, Citizenship Foundation.

Joyce, S. (1994) *Values Education Resource Book.* London, Ginn.

Keane, D. (1990) The Decade of the Citizen. *The Guardian*, 1 August.

Kerckhoff, A. C., Fogelman, K., Crook, D. and Reeder, D. (1996) *Going Comprehensive in England and Wales: a study of uneven change.* London, The Woburn Press.

Kinder, K., Harland, J. and Wootten, M. (1991) *The Impact of School-Focused INSET on Classroom Practice.* Slough, National Foundation for Educational Research.

Kragh, G. (1995) Education for Democracy, Social Justice, Respect for Human Rights and Global Responsibility: a psychological perspective, in Osler, A., Rathenow, H-F. and Starkey, H. (eds) *Teaching for Citizenship in Europe.* Stoke on Trent, Trentham Books.

Kymlicka, W. (1995) *Multicultural Citizenship.* Oxford, Oxford University Press.

Lamb, J. H., Nagin, D. S. and Sampson, R. J. (1998) Trajectories of Change in Criminal Offending: good marriages and the desistance process. *American Sociological Review*, 68, 225–38.

Laski, H. (1934) *Democracy in Crisis.* London, Allen & Unwin.

Lauriala, A. (1997) The Role of Practicum Contexts in Enhancing Change in Student Teacher Professional Beliefs. *European Journal of Teacher Education*, 20, 3, 267–82.

Lawn, M. (1996) *Modern Times? Work, Professionalism and Citizenship in Teaching*. London, Falmer Press.

Lawton, D. (1992) *Education and Politics in the 1990s: conflict or consensus?* London, Falmer Press.

Lee, P., Dickinson, A. and Ashby, R. (1996) 'There Were No Facts in Those Days': children's ideas about historical explanation, in Hughes, M. (ed.) *Teaching and Learning in Changing Times*. Oxford, Basil Blackwell.

Lister, I. (1984) *The Problem with Peace Studies*. Paper available from Department of Educational Studies, University of York.

Lloyd, J., Nixon, J. and Ranson, S. (1993) *Democracy Then and Now*. London, Heinemann.

Logue, P. (no date) *Speak Your Piece. Exploring Controversial Issues: a guide for teachers, youth and community workers*. Warwick, Channel 4.

Lyle, S. (1996) Environmental Education for Sustainable Futures: developing an action research model for primary initial teacher education, in Steiner, M. (ed.) *Developing the Global Teacher: theory and practice in initial teacher education*. Stoke on Trent, Trentham Books.

Marquand, D. (1997) *The New Reckoning: capitalism, states and citizens*. Cambridge, Polity Press.

Marshall, S. J. (1988) The Origins and Development of Political Education. *Teaching Politics*, 17, 1, 3–10.

Marshall, T. H. (1963) Citizenship and Social Class, in *Sociology at the Crossroads*. London, Heinemann.

Measham, F., Newcomb, R. and Parker, H. (1994) The Normalisation of Recreational Drug Use amongst Young People in North-west England. *British Journal of Sociology*, 45, 287–312.

Meighan, R. (1986) *A Sociology of Educating* (2nd edn). Eastbourne, Holt Education.

Mellor, S. and Elliott, S. (1996) *School Ethos and Citizenship*. Australian Council for Educational Research, Curriculum Corporation.

Ministry of Education (1947) *The New Secondary Education. Pamphlet No. 9*. London, HMSO.

Ministry of Education (1949) *Citizens Growing Up. Pamphlet No. 16*. London, HMSO.

Ministry of Education (1959) *15–17: A Report of the Central Advisory Council for Education, England, Vol 1*. (The Crowther Report). London, HMSO.

Ministry of Education (1963) *Half Our Future: A Report of the Central Advisory Council for Education, England* (The Newsom Report). London, HMSO.

Moletsane, R. (1998) Towards Democratic Teacher Education in South Africa: an exploratory case study, in Harber, C. (ed.) *Voices for Democracy: a north–south dialogue on education for sustainable democracy*. Nottingham, Education Now in association with the British Council.

Montgomery, A. and Smith, A. (1997) *Values in Education in Northern Ireland*. School of Education, University of Ulster.

Mulgan, G. (1990) The Buck Stops Here. *Marxism Today*, September.

NCC (National Curriculum Council) (1990) *Education for Citizenship. Curriculum Guidance 8*. York, NCC.

Newcastle upon Tyne Education Committee (undated) *The Nuclear Issue in Education: a teaching guide for Newcastle schools. Part one: the bomb*. Newcastle, Newcastle Education Committee.

References

Nichol, R. (1995) Citizenship Education and Teacher Preparation in Australia: an overview. Unpublished paper presented to the Department of Educational Studies, University of York, October 1995.

Nock, S. L. (1998) The Consequences of Pre-marital Fatherhood. *American Sociological Review*, 63, 250–63.

Nussbaum, M. (1997) *Cultivating Humanity: a classic defense of reform in liberal education*. Cambridge, MA, Harvard University Press.

Oakshott, M. (1956) Political Education, in Laslett, P. (ed.) *Philosophy, Politics and Society*. Oxford, Basil Blackwell.

O'Keefe, D. (1986) *The Wayward Curriculum: a cause for parents' concern?* London, The Social Affairs Unit.

Oliver, D. and Heater, D. (1994) *The Foundations of Citizenship*. London, Harvester Wheatsheaf.

Oliver, D. W. and Shaver, J. P. (1966) *Teaching Public Issues in the High School*. Boston, Houghton Mifflin Co.

Osler, A. and Starkey, H. (1996) *Teacher Education and Human Rights*. London, David Fulton.

Oxfam (1997) *A Curriculum for Global Citizenship*. London, Oxfam.

Paterson, L. (1998) The Civic Activism of Scottish Teachers: explanations and consequences. *Oxford Review of Education*, 24, 3, 279–302.

Pendry, A. and O'Neill, C. (1997) Research Agendas and History Teacher Educators, in Pendry, A. and O'Neill, C. (eds) *Principles and Practice: analytical perspectives on curriculum reform and changing pedagogy from history teacher educators*. Lancaster, Standing Conference of History Teacher Educators in the United Kingdom.

Phillips, R. (1997) Thesis and Antithesis in Tate's Views on History, Culture and Nationhood. *Teaching History*, 86, 30–4.

Pike, G. and Selby, D. (1988) *Global Teacher, Global Learner*. London, Hodder & Stoughton.

QCA (Qualifications and Curriculum Authority) (1998) *Education for Citizenship and the Teaching of Democracy in Schools* (The Crick Report). London, Qualifications and Curriculum Authority.

Rainer, J. and Guyton, E. (1999) Democratic Practices in Teacher Education and the Elementary Classroom. *Teaching and Teacher Education*, 15, 1, 121–32.

Rawls, J. (1993) *Political Liberalism*. New York, Columbia University Press.

Ree, H. (1973) *Educator Extraordinary: the life and achievements of Henry Morris*. London, Longman.

Reeher, G. and Cammarano, J. (eds) (1997) *Education for Citizenship: ideas and innovations in political learning*. Oxford, Rowman & Littlefield.

Reimer, E. (1975) *School is Dead: an essay on alternatives in education*. Harmondsworth, Penguin.

Rey, M. (1991) Migration and Intercultural Education: genealogical studies in teacher training, in Barkowski, H. and Hoff, G. R. (eds) *Berlin Interkulturell: Ergbnisse Einer Berliner Konferenz Zu Migration Und Padogogik*. Berlin, Wissenschaft und Stadt Colloquium Verlag.

Riley, S. C. (1996) Teacher Perceptions of the Qualities of Good Citizenship in Comprehensive Secondary Schools in England. Unpublished Ed.D. thesis, Seattle, Seattle Pacific University.

Rimmerman, C. A. (1997) *The New Citizenship: unconventional politics, activism and service*. Oxford, Westview Press.

Robson, P. J. (1996) *Forbidden Drugs*. Oxford, Oxford University Press.

Rorty, R. (1998) *Truth and Progress*. Cambridge, Cambridge University Press.

Ross, A. (1998) Children's Identity and Citizenship in Europe. Unpublished paper.

Rowe, D. and Newton, J. (1994) *You, Me, Us!* London, Home Office.

Ryan, C. (1996) Pedagogy and Practice in Primary Teacher Education for a European Dimension, in Veldhuis, R. and Ehmke, H. (eds) *Political Education towards a European Democracy*. Papers of a European conference held at Maastricht, October 1995, pp. 115–28.

Schools Council (1967) *Society and the Young School Leaver: a humanities programme in preparation for the raising of the school leaving age. Working paper No. 11.* London, HMSO.

Scruton, R. (1985) *World Studies: education as indoctrination*. London, Institute for European Defence and Strategic Studies.

Sell, L. and Robson, P. (1998) Perceptions of College Life, Emotional Well-being and Patterns of Drug and Alcohol Use among Oxford Undergraduates. *Oxford Review of Education*, 24, 2, 235–43.

Siraj-Blatchford, I. (1993) Social Justice and Teacher Education in the UK, in Verma, G. (ed.) *Inequality and Teacher Education: an international perspective*. London, Falmer Press.

Siraj-Blatchford, I. (1995) Little Citizens: helping children to help each other, in Siraj-Blatchford, J. and Siraj-Blatchford, I. (eds) *Educating the Whole Child*. Buckingham, Open University Press.

The Spectator (1993) Look and Learn. *The Spectator*, 27 February.

Steiner, M. (ed.) (1996) *Developing the Global Teacher: theory and practice in initial teacher education*. Stoke on Trent, Trentham Books.

Stewart, M. (1938) *Bias and Education for Democracy*. Oxford, Oxford University Press.

Stradling, R. (1977) *The Political Awareness of the School Leaver*. London, Hansard Society.

Stradling, R. (1984) *Teaching Controversial Issues*. London, Edward Arnold.

Stradling, R. (1987) Political Education and Politicization in Britain: a ten-year retrospective. Paper Presented at the International Round Table Conference of the Research Committee on Political Education of the International Political Science Association. Ostkolleg der Bundeszentrale fur Politische Bildung, Köln, 9–13 March.

Stradling, R. and Noctor, M. (1981) *The Provision of Political Education*. London, Curriculum Review Unit.

Tapper, T. and Salter, B. (1979) Book review of Crick, B. and Porter, A. (eds) *Political Education and Political Literacy* in *International Journal of Political Education*, 2, 93–5.

Tate, N. (1997) Education for Citizenship. Speech at a conference organized by the Secondary Heads' Association, the Hansard Society and the Citizenship Foundation. Leicester, September.

Tate, N. (1998) It's Good to Listen. *The Times Educational Supplement*, 29 May, p. 15.

Trafford, B. (1997) *Participation, Power-sharing and School Improvement*. Nottingham, Educational Heretics Press.

References

Turner, B. (ed.) (1993) *Citizenship and Social Theory*. London, Sage.

UNICEF (1990) *The Rights of the Child*. London, UNICEF.

Voiels, V. (1996) The Inner Self and Becoming A Teacher, in Steiner, M. (ed.) *Developing the Global Teacher: theory and practice in initial teacher education*. Stoke on Trent, Trentham Books.

Whitmarsh, G. (1974) The Politics of Political Education: an episode. *Journal of Curriculum Studies*, 6, 2, 133–42.

Whitty, G., Rowe, G. and Aggleton, P. (1994) Subjects and Themes in the Secondary School Curriculum. *Research Papers in Education*, 9, 2, 159–81.

Whitty, G., Aggleton, P. and Rowe, G. (1996): Competing Conceptions of Quality in Social Education: learning from the experience of cross-curricular themes, in M. Hughes, M. (ed.) *Teaching and Learning in Changing Times*. Oxford, Basil Blackwell.

Wringe, C. (1998) Education for Citizenship beyond the Nation State: Europe and the world. *Talking Politics*, 11, 1, 17–20.

Index